"Jani Ortlund writes with passion—passion to be God's instrument to woo or cajole our society back to health again. And if any book was ever autobiographical, this is it! She lives her passions. Listen to a woman who is fearlessly feminine, and then ask God to move in your life to make you the same."

ANNE ORTLUND, AUTHOR, *DISCIPLINES OF THE BEAUTIFUL WOMAN* AND *I WANT TO SEE YOU, LORD*

"Jani Ortlund's perspective on womanhood is compelling and refreshing. Her book is chock-full of personal anecdotes and practical advice that is 'tried, tested, and true.' Read her challenge, boldly embrace God's plan—if you dare, and fall in love with your destiny as a woman!"

MARY KASSIAN. PRESIDENT, ALABASTER FLASK MINISTRIES

"Jani Ortlund challenges us to fearlessly face our culture's distortions of womanhood and to dismantle them with biblical truth. This engaging and practical book reads like a warm conversation with a very wise and godly woman. How refreshing and how right!"

SUSAN HUNT, DIRECTOR OF WOMEN IN THE CHURCH MINISTRY, PRESBYTERIAN CHURCH IN AMERICA CHRISTIAN EDUCATION COMMITTEE

Fearlessly Feminine

Boldly Living

God's Plan

for Womanhood

By

JANI ORTLUND

Multnomah®Publishers *Sisters, Oregon*

FEARLESSLY FEMININE

published by Multnomah Publishers, Inc.

© 2000 Jani Ortlund

International Standard Book Number: 1–57673–669–5

Cover image by Zephyr Images
Design by Stephen Gardner

Scripture quotations are from:
The Holy Bible, New International Version (NIV)
© 1973, 1978, 1984 by International Bible Society,
used by permission of Zondervan Publishing House.

Multnomah is a trademark of Multnomah Publishers, Inc.,
and is registered in the U.S. Patent and Trademark Office.
The colophon is a trademark of Multnomah Publishers, Inc.

Printed in the United States of America

For information:
MULTNOMAH PUBLISHERS, INC.
POST OFFICE BOX 1720
SISTERS, OREGON 97759

Library of Congress Cataloging–in–Publication Data
Ortlund, Jani.
   Fearlessly feminine : boldly living God's plan for womanhood / by Jani
Ortlund.   p.cm.   ISBN 1-57673-669-5 (pbk.)
   1. Christian women–Religious life.   I. Title.
   BV4527.O79 2000   248.8'43–dc21   99-050998

00 01 02 03 04 05 06 — 10 9 8 7 6 5 4 3 2 1 0

To Jeanne Osborn Giles

tender caregiver, patient teacher, beloved mother
Thank you

Like Sarah, who obeyed Abraham and called him
her master. You are her daughters if you do what
is right and do not give way to fear.

I PETER 3:6

Contents

Preface

The purpose of this book is to draw women to God. It is about God and you. It is a book that is meant to help you enjoy being a woman. Its message will enhance your femininity. It will show you how God can help you to be *fearlessly* feminine in all areas of your life. It will encourage you so to trust God that you will do anything for His blessing and glory.

It is also about me. I could not write about being a woman without opening my heart and life to you. This book has emerged out of counseling and speaking experiences with women through years of ministry with my husband. As those experiences grew, I grew with them. I hope that what God has done to encourage me in fearless femininity will also encourage you.

This book is about you and me and what God has given us in common—our feminine souls. What does it mean to be a woman? Why is it so important that we be fearless? I want to talk about that with you as we couple fearlessness with femininity. I want to call Christian women to be joyfully confident in who we are before God. I want us to fearlessly embrace the privilege of womanhood and show the world the beauty of Christian femininity for God's glory.

And so this book. My prayer is that God will use it to nurture and beautify His daughters as we seek to further His kingdom here on earth.

Jani Ortlund
Augusta, Georgia

Charm is deceptive, and beauty is fleeting;
*but a woman who fears the L*ORD *is to be praised.*

PROVERBS 31:30

Nothing to Fear, Nothing to Regret
PANDITA RAMABAI
(1858–1922)

As a young girl in India, Ramabai was instructed in Sanskrit and the sacred Puranas by her mother and father. She spent her childhood wandering from village to village with her Hindu parents. At the age of eighteen she watched her father, mother, and sister starve to death. She then moved to Calcutta and began teaching Sanskrit among reform-minded Hindus, but was accused by the orthodox religious establishment of destroying Hinduism and the Indian family, because they opposed women who knew and taught their sacred writings.

When her husband of nineteen months died of cholera, she was left totally alone to care for their infant daughter. In 1882 she began her great work for India's ostracized and abused widows, battling for their care and for the prohibition of child marriages. While studying in England the following year, she observed the difference between Christians and Hindus.

"After my visit to the Homes at Fulham, I began to think there was a real difference between Hinduism and Christianity.... I realized, after reading the 4th Chapter of St. John's Gospel, that Christ was truly the Divine Saviour He claimed to be, and no one but He could transform and uplift the downtrodden womanhood of India and of every land." [1] She was baptized and then came to the U.S. to study, write, and raise funds to establish homes for young Hindu widows.

Returning to India in 1889, she became one of her country's great liberators, freeing thousands of widows and orphans from the curse they were suffering under Hinduism. Amidst great political opposition and physical deprivation she began meeting the needs of hundreds of young women and girls. By 1900 she had over nineteen hundred people under her care. She had to feed and house them, educate them, teach them trades, find them jobs, and arrange their marriages. Her days began at 4:00 A.M. and often lasted late into the night.

She learned Greek and Hebrew and worked hard on a vernacular Bible translation. Through it all, God was her joy and her strength. "I feel very happy," she wrote, "since the Lord called me to step out in faith, and I obeyed. We are not rich, nor great, but we are happy, getting our daily bread from the loving hands of our Heavenly Father, having not a *pice* (Indian coin) over and above our daily necessities, having no banking account anywhere, no endowment or income from any earthly source, but depending altogether on our Father God; we have nothing to fear from anybody, nothing to lose, and nothing to regret. The Lord is our Inexhaustible Treasure."[2]

CHAPTER ONE

Feminine Fears and Faith

Our premarital counseling session with the earnest young seminary couple was coming to a close. Although he had been raised in a loving Christian environment from birth, her story was different. She described to us what it was like to be raised by a mother who had divorced twice and then moved in with a female lover. No wonder this new believer asked me as we finished up our time together, "What does it mean to be a truly Christian woman? I've never seen it up close, and frankly, it scares me."

How my heart ached for her and for others we had worked with through the years. Their doubts and questions and fears cry out for an answer—an answer full of the all-sufficiency of Christ. Our God-given femininity has been assaulted in recent decades, and we have begun to wonder what it means to be a woman. Our role as women has become muddled and distorted, giving rise to false stereotypes of femininity. Confusion has set in.

The Spirit of Femininity

Who are we as women before God? Femininity is more extensive and substantial and far-reaching and significant than could adequately be discussed in a single book, so our exploration of the topic will not be exhaustive. But I want you to take away a sense of how God sees you as a woman. What is His design for you? What does it mean to be a woman and not a man? What should direct our feminine responses to life?

John Piper in *Recovering Biblical Manhood and Womanhood* defines femininity this way:

> At the heart of mature femininity is a freeing disposition to affirm, receive, and nurture strength and leadership from worthy men in ways appropriate to a woman's differing relationships.[3]

I like how Piper describes femininity as a *disposition*, an attitude, an inclination. To define femininity is not to lay out a set of rules or behaviors, because differing situations and relationships will call for various responses. Femininity will not look the same in all women. Nor will it always express itself the same way toward all men. Our femininity will take on different shapes and flavors as it is expressed toward a son or a husband or an employer or an employee or a salesman or a pastor or a father. But true femininity, fearless femininity, will always seek to express itself in appropriate, godly ways as we nurture, affirm, and receive the resources of masculinity surrounding us.

And our femininity is not expressed only toward men. It will shape and affect our relationships with everyone we interact with, including our mothers and daughters and coworkers and sisters and friends and neighbors. Throughout our lives, God calls us to respond to those around us—men and women, boys and girls—as true women of God.

Many women today are confused about what it means to be feminine. The distinctions between men and woman are growing hazy. A young woman recently told me of her experiences with some modeling agencies. After being encouraged by professionals she knew to try modeling, she interviewed at a few agencies in a major U.S. city. Although the managers of these agencies were very polite, they let this beautiful young woman know that her figure was too classic (i.e., womanly) for the current unisex look. Fortunately, this young lady loves being a woman and is happy to seek other employment. But we both found it sad that the distinctions between men and women are no longer being honored and enjoyed as our culture works at erasing the fine lines of femininity in the name of equality.

What We Fear

This confusion that we see and feel around us often breeds fear. Some women are fearful that they might miss out if they embrace God's design for them as women. They fear they will not experience self-fulfillment or gain the respect of their families and communities. Yet they wonder what to do with the longings deep in their souls for love and meaningful relationships and a desire for significance.

Fear is a complex emotion. It can fuel us so that we strive harder to succeed. Or it can freeze us, so that we stay home eating cookie dough and reading the latest gossip magazines. Women today struggle with many fears:

- We fear the embarrassment of failure, and we fear the pressures of success.
- We fear the vulnerability of giving ourselves to another, and we fear the ache of loneliness.
- We fear the stress of working outside the home, and we fear the boredom of staying at home full-time.
- We fear marriage, and we fear being single.
- We fear pregnancy, and we fear infertility.
- We fear the responsibility of raising children, and we fear the emptiness of not investing in the next generation.
- We fear appearing immature, and we fear growing old.
- We fear the past, and we fear the future.
- We fear the restraints of biblical femininity, and we fear missing out on the joys of true womanhood.

But most of all, we fear the sacrifices that being a woman of godly character demands.

The Failures of Fear

The problem with fear is that it works so well. It motivates and influences us. It coerces us to conform. It drives us to compete. It prods us to perform. Fear has been a part of our feminine hearts since the Garden of Eden. When Eve took the fruit and ate it, she was motivated by fear—fear that she would miss out on what was "good...and pleasing...and also desirable" (Genesis 3:6); fear that God didn't really have her best interests in mind; fear that obedience would exact too high a price. And we have been assaulted by our fears ever since. I want to confront some of our feminine fears in this book.

Our natural instincts turn life inside out. When troubles

come, we doubt God and His care, and before we know it, we give way to our fears. Rather than a trembling, joyful fear that bows humbly before God, we feel a trembling, crushing fear that runs from Him. Along with Eve, we hear Satan whispering in our hearts, "Did God really say?" (Genesis 3:1). And so we fret and eat and fantasize and take things into our own hands. We make self the center of our lives, and God becomes some peripheral religious ornamentation, all in a fear-driven attempt to secure our happiness.

But does it work? Are we happy? Look at the world. Look at all the abortions and divorces and troubled children. Look at the rejections and regrets and remorse. We only want to be happy. So why aren't we? Because we believe a lie. We believe we'll be happy when everything is finally going our way. But this is a deception. What we really need is not a perfect life with everything we crave neatly assembled around us. What we really need is God.

If our hearts cling to that picture-perfect existence, we will fear not attaining it. And if in some small way we find ourselves beginning to attain it, we will fear losing it. But God does not want us to live in fear. God wants to drive out our fears with His love. He tells us in 1 John 4:18 that "There is no fear in love. But perfect love drives out fear." What does this look like? How can we get free from the grip of fear? What is the answer to our fears?

The answer to fear is not more self-control. The answer to fear is not withdrawal. The answer to fear is not even drumming up more courage. Fear and courage can coexist in a woman's heart. In fact, fear may even sharpen our courage. The fear of divorce gives us the courage to hang in there through the rough times. The fear of failure in front of our coworkers gives us the courage to pay the price in the market place. The fear of being thought of as a nobody gives us the courage to work a little harder and a little longer to prove ourselves.

My fears are many—they revolve around my family and their needs, my ministries and their demands, and especially right now about this book and its completion. What fears are assailing you as you read?

Fear is a hard taskmaster. It leaves us exhausted and drained, uncertain and off balance. It keeps us looking over our shoulders for the next trial to begin, wondering if we'll have enough inner reserve to carry on. Fear is self-perpetuating. It grows as we feed it with time and attention. Fear is the chief enemy of the feminine soul. It robs us of our ability to nurture those around us. Fear thwarts our receptivity. It intercepts our love for others. It debilitates our faith. It is Satan's trap, binding us to self-absorption.

God's Answer to Our Fears

So what is God's answer to our fears? His answer is *faith.* What can conquer our fears without wiping out our courage? Only faith can. The opposite of fear is faith—and not just some nebulous good feeling about fate or good fortune. Real faith, real fear-shrinking faith, comes from a personal, vibrant, satisfying relationship with the God who is more than a match for anything that intimidates us.

Jesus said, "Peace I leave with you; my peace I give you. I do not give to you as the world gives. Do not let your hearts be troubled and *do not be afraid*" (John 14:27, italics mine). The prophet Isaiah wrote, "So *do not fear,* for I am with you; *do not be dismayed,* for I am your God. I will strengthen you and help you; I will uphold you with my righteous right hand" (Isaiah 41:10, italics mine). Faith in a perfect, personal, peace-giving, and strength-increasing God is what drives out our fears and frees us to be fearlessly feminine.

What fears are absorbing your time and energy right now? Are you frightened by poor health? Financial uncertainties? A troubled marriage? Gnawing fatigue? An uncertain future? Broken relationships? An overwhelming grief? Rebellious children? What is your response to the inevitable difficulties of life? Fear is not necessarily a sin, although it certainly can lead us to sin. The vital thing is that you "not give way to fear" (1 Peter 3:6). Your response to your fears proves to whom you look for strength and help and stability under the pressures of this life.

God has placed within each of us a soul. And the human soul is so vast. It is more vast, more profound, than the world and all that it contains. That's why there is nothing in this world that can ultimately satisfy us—not money or marriage or children or beauty or power or respect or love or success or anything else you can think of. Only God in Christ has the fullness to match this vastness and bring ease and contentment and rest to our souls. "My soul finds rest *in God alone*" (Psalm 62:1, italics mine).

The Restless Soul

Our souls are restless. We long for rest in our inner beings. We know that God is the one to whom we ought to bring our fears, but we feel a tension between ourselves and God. The Bible says there are only two kinds of people on earth: those who are alienated from God and are forever restless in their souls and those whose souls have found their rest in God.

To be able to deal with our restlessness we have to know where it comes from. The root of our restlessness is sin. We must understand what sin really is if we are to be fearlessly feminine. What marks the human race, every one of us without exception, is our evil. We don't want to believe that. We like to think of ourselves as having things under control. When we blow it, there is a perfectly justifiable reason. We like to see ourselves as nice people who make bad choices, good people who make the occasional, understandable mistake. But the Bible tells us that we are evil people proving what we really are. There are no exceptions (Romans 3:10–12).

Sin is not just making mistakes. Sin is not just doing bad things. Sin touches a person's very nature. We are not nice people who sometimes mess up. We are evil people proving what we really are. Sin colors everything we think and do and say. You and I are dominated by sin, warped by sin, so deeply biased by sin that we live under its control, its consequences, and ultimately its condemnation. I wonder if we really believe that? We live in a day that tells us to concentrate on the good things about ourselves, to develop positive self-images. But we must hear and believe what God says about us. We cannot continue to justify ourselves with such excuses as fatigue or family background or ignorance. That self-justifying impulse is what causes our alienation from God.

You may be thinking, *Jani, you don't understand. I am not a bad person. I go to church. I vote. I don't litter. I volunteer at our local nursing home. I try to be good.* But how good is good enough? Where do you draw the line? More importantly, where does God draw the line?

Crossing the Line

The line God draws is very clear. He demands *perfection,* and no one has ever measured up. The Bible says that the restlessness we feel, the doubts and fears about life and eternity, come from being alienated from God. Paul tells us in Romans 3:10–12, "There is no one righteous, not even one; there is no one who understands, no one who seeks God. All have turned away, they have together become worthless; there is no one who does good, not even one." How can we live happily here in God's world when we're not at peace with God Himself? How can we feel comfortable as His guests when there is unresolved tension between ourselves and our host? Until we know peace with God, we'll never know peace within.

We try to ease that tension, each in our own way. We try being extra good, making new resolutions, bargaining with God. We try the comparison game: "Well, I may not be as good as Mother Teresa, but I am certainly better than *her!*" Some of us even try to turn the tables on God to make Him look bad. We blame Him and turn our failings into an argument that God is too demanding or unfair. We think that if God were *really* trustworthy, He would act more like we think He should.

Have you ever thought, "If God were *really* kind (or loving or merciful or powerful—you fill in the blank), He would act *this* way." Do you find yourself wondering, *How could God do that?* You doubt Him because He doesn't conform to your definition of God. This will never bring peace. It will never ease the tension between God and you.

Your restlessness can only be calmed and satisfied as you bow before God and let Him call all the shots. All defensiveness will stop when you allow God to be God. A Christian steps across the line to take God's side. There is a trembling, joyful fear that bows humbly before the Lord, yielding to Him the authentic obedience that comes from faith. Proverbs 19:23 tells us that *this* kind of fear "leads to life. Then one rests content, untouched by trouble." And this wonderful response, which the Bible calls fearing God, will also bring good to those around you. Jeremiah 32:39 says, "I will give them singleness of heart and action, so that they will always fear me for their own good and the good of their children after them."

To be reconciled to God, to step across that line, you must lay down all your defensiveness. You must let God be God. Don't remake Him into your own self-serving deity. That is idolatry. Don't wait to trust Him until He responds in the way you think He should. That is self-centeredness. Don't dictate the terms to God. That is His prerogative. When you see God as He really is, all excuses are silenced.

God has provided a place for you to give Him all your excuses and defensiveness. There is a place where you can confess your sin and find peace with God. There is a place that calls you to step across the line. That place is at the foot of the cross of Jesus Christ, God's only Son. The cross is where you can find rest for your soul, peace with God, freedom from fear. The Bible says:

> For God was pleased to have all his fullness dwell in him, and through him to reconcile to himself all things, whether things on earth or things in heaven, by making peace through His blood, shed on the cross. Once you were alienated from God and were enemies in your minds because of your evil behavior. But now he has reconciled you by Christ's physical body

through death to present you holy in his sight, without blemish and free from accusation. (Colossians 1:19–22)

The cross is the place of God's peace for us. It is the place of quiet and rest and reconciliation. It is here that God's grace washes over sinners who have nothing to say to God in their favor. Christ presents us to God, unstained and cleared of any charges against us, because of the divine arrangement He and His Father made at the cross.

Dread or Delight at the Cross of Christ

Have you come to this place yet? Will you assume the best of God and the worst of yourself? No more challenging God. No more insisting that God defend Himself. Step across the line to take God's side. Let God be God to you. This is what it means to be a Christian. My husband put it this way in a recent sermon, "Trust God enough to let Him be all that He is to you. Don't accept an edited version of God, whittled down and rendered manageable. Delight and dread are the two fundamental states of mind before God. And every one of us is gravitating in one direction or the other. The fork in the road is at the cross of Jesus."[4]

Maybe you have never come to that fork before. But you're there now. Let God give you a new beginning. He loves you. He wants to ease that restlessness in your soul with His very presence. Lay your sins at the fork in the road and turn down the pathway of delight. Repent of your own willfulness and self-absorption. Receive, embrace, and enjoy God's gift to you. Make the gift of His Son your personal treasure. You will never be fearlessly feminine until you disown yourself and replace your fears with faith in Christ. Then your fears will give way to peace, as Isaiah the prophet tells us, "You will keep in perfect peace him whose mind is steadfast, because he trusts in you. Trust in the LORD forever, for the LORD, the LORD, is the Rock eternal" (Isaiah 26:3–4). Through Christ you can have peace with God, beginning right now and stretching on forever.

Or maybe you are already a Christian, traveling down the pathway of delightful rest in Christ. But your delight has been diminished in the shadow of fear. Perhaps you have bought into our culture's esteem of self and have sought rest for your soul in the wrong places. Come back. Find your solace in Christ alone. Discover the joy of Christ-centeredness.[5] Trust Him so much that you are delivered from bondage to yourself. In Christ you will find everything worth trusting and enjoying and spending yourself for.

Daughters of Sarah

Abraham's wife, Sarah, could have lived her life in the shadow of fear. She struggled with many of the fears women have faced through the ages: infertility, moving from a familiar to an unknown place, a husband who asked difficult—even wrong—things of her, jealousy and conflict among the members of her household (see Genesis chapters 12–23). Yet she *would not let her fears dominate her.* She trusted in God, and He honored her for it. Her name is mentioned in the Bible more than any other woman's. When Peter wanted to teach us how to be pure and reverent and beautiful, he used Sarah as an example.

For this is the way the holy women of the past who put their hope in God used to make themselves beauti- ful. They were submissive to their own husbands, like Sarah, who obeyed Abraham and called him her mas- ter. You are her daughters if you do what is right and do not give way to fear. (1 Peter 3:5–6)

Sarah never had any biological daughters, but she has many spiritual daughters. And we are her daughters if, like Sarah, we accept that the most important thing in life is to do what is right, without giving way to fear. To be fearlessly femi- nine means to affirm and receive and nurture those God brings to us. It means to trust Him enough to let Him be God in our lives (Luke 1:38).

None of us knows what this life holds for us. Sarah didn't. The first mention of her in Scripture rings with a sadness that only a woman can fully comprehend: "Now Sarai was barren; she had no children" (Genesis 11:30). But God has given her many spiritual daughters through the ages. The last time she appears in the Bible, we read of her enduring legacy: "You are her daughters if you do what is right and do not give way to fear" (1 Peter 3:6). Be a daughter of Sarah. Boldly follow her out of the shadow of your fears.

I do not know what fears assault your heart today. You know. God knows. He wants to take those fears away and replace them with peace as you trust in Him. He is the one who is able to help you live in loveliness and serenity because "the Lord of peace" is with you, and He will "give you peace at all times and in every way" (2 Thessalonians 3:16). Let Him help you fall in love with your destiny as a woman. Let Him replace your fears with a dignified confidence of mind and heart.

God through Christ is able to make us women who do not look for fulfillment in our homes or our careers or our bodies or the achievements of our children or our talents or our brains. He is able to make us women who find ourselves in Him. He wants to replace our fears with faith in Him. His plan for us is good and pleasing and perfect. Let us trust God enough to leave our whiny self-absorption behind and look to Him. He will make us vital Christian women who demonstrate the beauty and power of Christ. He will help us match the moment in which we live. He will make us fearlessly feminine.

Study Questions

1. What fears crowd your heart?

2. In what ways, apart from God, do you seek rest from your fears?

3. Describe your relationship with God. Is there tension there?

4. Have you found peace with God through Christ your Savior? If not, why not now?

5. Read 1 Peter 3:5–6 and 2 Thessalonians 3:16. How can you best match the moment in which you live with fearless femininity?

To say that if you don't like the popular culture, then turn it off, is like saying if you don't like the smog, stop breathing.

Esther Experiences
KAY COLES JAMES
(1949–)

F or the past twenty years Kay James has been active in the analysis, development, and implementation of American public policy. She is a frequent commentator and lecturer on a variety of domestic policy issues. She currently serves as Senior Fellow for the Citizenship Project at the Heritage Foundation, where she helps lead Heritage's effort to restore a strong ethic of citizenship and civic responsibility. She is also Dean of the School of Government at Regent University in Virginia Beach, Virginia.

How did this warm, articulate, and compassionate woman rise above her extremely rough beginning? She was one of six children born into poverty to a loving mother and an alcoholic, abusive father. Her aunt and uncle took her in at age four and gave her opportunities that her mother, who remained close to Kay, couldn't provide. While watching a televised Billy Graham Crusade her senior year in high school, she committed her life to Christ. During her four years at Hampton University in Virginia, she learned to love God and His Word through attending campus Bible studies.

Since college, she has served in many capacities, both public and private:

- Senior Vice President for The Family Research Council in Washington, D.C.
- Associate Director for the White House Office of National Drug Control Policy and Assistant Secretary for Public Affairs at the U.S. Department of Health and Human Resources (both under President Bush)

- Former chairman of the National Gambling Impact Study Commission
- Commissioner of the National Commission on Children, appointed by President Reagan
- Public Affairs Director for the National Right to Life Committee
- A member of such boards as Focus on the Family, Young Life, Women to the World, International, and the Fairfax County and Virginia State Boards of Education

Despite her extensive political responsibilities, Kay's chief commitment is to her family. "I say unashamedly that my top priorities are my husband and my kids. If you want to deal with Kay James, you've got to deal with that reality."[1]

She says that you can have it all—career and family—but just not at the same time. She was at home for almost nine years when her three children were young. When the kids went to school, she started volunteer work, which gradually evolved into more. She has authored two books: her autobiography, *Never Forget*, in 1993, and *Transforming America from the Inside Out*, in 1995.

Kay James believes there are certain things on which you should never compromise, no matter what the consequences. As a pro-life media spokesperson she has had to take a lot of heat. How does she respond? "I think we all have to get to the point where we have our 'Esther experience,' when we decide to go before the King with what is right, and if we perish, we perish."[2]

CHAPTER TWO

Playing with Popular Culture

~~~~~

It was a normal Sunday evening service at our church—that is, until the bird flew into the sanctuary. When it flew in, all normalcy flew out. The primary choir, which had just finished singing, started pointing and giggling. There were nervous coughs and shuffles as the congregation tried to discern the proper response to our newest visitor. And my dear Ray, while at the pulpit, was baffled as to how to remove this distraction from our midst.

The bird was having quite a grand time of it, flitting from chandelier to candelabra to choir loft in our thirty-foot-high sanctuary. We either had to cancel the service or ignore the bird, and we chose the latter—but with little success. Finally, during one of the hymns, the bird flew into a recessed light in the choir loft. After a few seconds it suddenly dropped straight down and landed with a soft thud near the organ, where two of our alert deacons slipped in and removed it.

Like that bird, the effects of popular culture have flown into the church, causing a distraction impossible to ignore. Its flight from issue to issue has captivated us and diverted our attention from our God-blessed calling as women. Sometimes out of curiosity, other times out of fear or ignorance, we have toyed with the enticements of popular culture because we lack the discernment and confidence to evaluate them for what they are. And now we are left wondering why our lives echo with the hollow sadness of divorce, disappointment, and depression.

What Our Culture Honors

In recent times we have changed how we define our female heroes. When I was a child in the fifties, a woman was honored and revered if she gave herself to her husband and children. She was esteemed and admired because of her willing sacrifice for those she loved. She was encouraged to yield to her maternal yearnings, care for her husband, maintain her home, and devote herself to her children. These values now, however, are despised by some as meritless and backward, or at least dismissed as limited achievements compared with the satisfaction of earning a regular paycheck and being given power and respect outside the home.

Carolyn Graglia, in her book *Domestic Tranquility,* lays out for us the cultural assault on marriage, motherhood, and traditional sexuality that is rooted in the pursuit of political and economic power.

What were once considered valuable and respected activities—raising children, attending to a husband's needs, and managing a household—the present society created by contemporary feminism views as benighted and beyond rational justification. No woman with a brain in her head, feminists have largely convinced society, could possibly be happy devoting herself to what they portray as worthless, even degrading activities. No woman, as Justice Ginsburg implied, would willingly live a life of such limited achievement.[3]

It is safe to say that the feminist movement bears significant responsibility for dishonoring a woman if she makes her family her primary calling. As one critic explains:

Feminism is not about giving women freedom to choose; it is about taking away choices of which feminists disapprove. And one choice they disapprove of is participation in a conventional family.... Perhaps the most vicious aspect of radical feminism is that it necessarily criticizes and demeans women who choose to work primarily as mothers and homemakers.[4]

The women's movement has tried to ease a mother's guilt if she decides to leave her children and home and give herself to the marketplace. Look at some of the recent book titles on this subject:

• Diane Eyer, *Mother Infant Bonding: A Scientific Fiction,* 1993
• Joan Peters, *When Mothers Work: Loving Our Children without Sacrificing Ourselves,* 1997
• Susan Chira, *A Mother's Place: Taking the Debate about Working Mothers beyond Guilt and Blame,* 1998

The Sanctity of Self

Almost anything done in the name of a woman's independence is celebrated as raw courage. Women are seen to be more intelligent if they value a life of autonomy as richer and fuller than that of a homemaker. The cover of Dr. Wayne Dyer's book, *Your Erroneous Zones,* says it like this: "Dyer shows that *only you can make yourself happy,* and points the way to true *self-reliance*" (italics mine). Over and over again, we are encouraged to set our own rules, to define our own terms. Through TV commercials and sitcoms and talk shows, through books and movies, through speeches and political movements, we've been told that true happiness comes when we learn to enhance our self-respect apart from any connection with others, even those we should naturally love the most. We live in a day where personal *desires* take precedence over personal *ideals*. We've become more and more absorbed in ourselves and our sensations. We do that by putting ourselves first and glorifying our desires—emotional and sexual and material—thinking if it feels good, then that makes it good.

Living in this atmosphere of selfism, we're continually looking in the mirror, making lifetime choices on how we want to shape the reflection staring back at us. Contemporary culture ridicules any reflection of the traditional wife and mother devoted to her family, which in turn breeds an antipathy toward family life. It hardly seems the ambition of movie makers and TV producers to honor the traditional family and celebrate a stay-at-home mother's loving sacrifice for her children and husband. The cultural support structure for full-time homemaking has collapsed. Our self-absorption has bred increased rates of illegitimate births, institutional child rearing, abortion on demand, and divorce.[5] The thoroughly acculturated woman walking into the new millennium answers to no one but herself. She wants to be free, independent, self-confident, and unimpeded—especially by men.

The sanctity of self has permeated all aspects of our modern life, but I am particularly sensitive to how it has influenced the education of our children. When I taught public school, I was surprised at some of the children's literature that had risen to popularity. During my master's course work in education, we were admonished not to use the traditional family as a role model because for many students it was passé. Certain books were acclaimed as authoritative reading in the elementary classroom to teach children a modern perspective on women's issues. I found them, in some cases, offensive. They denigrated romance and love, manhood and womanhood, so that the sweet appeared bitter and the bitter sweet. Rather than being a glad celebration of womanhood, they portrayed an acidic, ugly attack on men.

"Elizabeth was a beautiful princess. She lived in a castle and had expensive clothes. She was going to marry a prince named Ronald" is how *The Paper Bag Princess* by Robert N. Munsch begins.[6] In this story a dragon smashes Elizabeth's castle, burns all her clothes, and carries off Ronald. Clothed in just a paper bag, she decides to chase the dragon and get Ronald back. Showing tremendous courage, cleverness, and strength, she plays upon the dragon's arrogance to get him to perform great feats of strength and speed. Finally, worn out from his braggadocio, he falls asleep. Elizabeth then enters the dragon's castle and rescues Ronald, who spurns her because of her paper bag attire. Not to be outdone, the story ends with her saying, "Ronald, you look like a real prince, but you are a bum."

Now Ronald *did* spurn Elizabeth. That wasn't *nice*. But this ideal of female autonomy and the denigration of a happy, selfless romance and marriage between a man and a woman opposes fearless femininity. The woman is portrayed as always being in charge, and the man is a petty, superficial jerk. This in-your-face attitude is offensive.

Within the larger backdrop of our divorce culture, some children's books portray marriage as a trap. "Princess Smartypants" was a beautiful, rich princess, who did not want to get married because she enjoyed being a Ms. and wanted to do exactly as she pleased.[7] When her parents insisted that she marry, she set impossible tasks which made all of her suitors look like fools. Just when she felt "safe," Prince Swashbuckle turned up and completed all her nearly-impossible requirements. Instead of keeping her promise, she gave him a magic kiss that turned him into a gigantic, warty toad. The book ends, "When the other princes heard what had happened to Prince Swashbuckle, none of them wanted to marry Smartypants...so she lived happily ever after."

The message comes through loud and clear: Happiness is found in doing exactly as we please. What kind of heroine is this for our young children? What does this teach them about marriage? Ought we really to avoid men at any cost? Is autonomy the goal we want our daughters to pursue?

What Our Culture Trivializes

The feminist mindset minimizes the differences between men and women in the gender-blending games it invites us to play. We have been led to think that our sexual differences are trivial and that casual, loveless sex is normal. But deep within, true women know how very different they are from their male counterparts and how beautiful the union of those differences can be. The inner longings and passions of women—the desire to be loved and cherished and to leave a legacy for the next generation—haven't changed. Fortunately, the desires of true womanhood, honored and nourished in previous generations, are still finding their way to the surface today as godly young women courageously embrace their fearless femininity.

Women who want to trust in God may have to work through feelings of intimidation. When our daughter, Krista, was a freshman in college, she was undecided about which major to choose. She confided in me that her deepest longing was to marry a godly man and serve Christ with him, hopefully raising children to carry on this vision in the next generation. "Mom," she said, "I know that you and Dad have sacrificed to send me to college. Will you think that I'm wasting all that money if I get married and spend my life serving my family rather than seeking a career?" I assured her that nothing could make us happier than to see her answer God's calling for her as a woman. We would be thrilled to see her excel as a wife and mother.

What is it that makes young women feel ill at ease about expressing their God-given yearning to make a home and bear and nurture children? It is all the feedback with which we nourish their dreams. We must not let the patterns of this world play havoc in the hearts of our future mothers and homemakers. Let's help nourish the fundamental God-instilled desires that feminism calls into question.

We may be more liberated as women now, but at what price? We're more strident, abrasive, loud, and lonely. And we're less happy, secure, dignified, and romanced. Our most destructive problems as women do not arise from inequality and sexism. Our most destructive problems spring from arrogant self-promotion, nervous self-preservation, and ignorance of God's Word to us. We worship what feels good. We seek escapist entertainment regardless of how it darkens our spirits. Rather than honor the eternal truth of God, we bow to the influences that shape worldly values. We expose our souls to the vulgarities of Hollywood. We become engrossed in its crudities and are titillated by its rumors. We degrade ourselves with gossip magazines from the checkout stand, videos that taint our purity, and soap operas that feed our fantasies. Thoughtless boredom can lead us to these diversions. Why should we allow the media, which shows little moral or spiritual restraint, to hold such influence over us? This is the opposite of fearless femininity.

We also have become utilitarian. We honor what is most useful or helpful to attain our goals. Therefore, if something is serviceable for one generation, fine; but if it doesn't fit the next, then discard it. If the goal is to build a beautiful home and live the American dream, and that necessitates a mother leaving her babies with a stranger so that she can climb the pay scale to afford vacations and remodeling and luxury vehicles, then the end justifies the means. But are truth and the past really as expendable as we think? What is *true* about being a woman? What connects us with every other female since Eve? What does God, the One who created us female, say to us *through the ages?*

God Honors Self-Sacrifice

We women have a God-given vocation that only fearless women can fulfill. We must take a stand against error in our generation. We must lift high the truths of Holy Scripture. God calls us to be mediators of truth and wisdom (Proverbs 31:26).

He wants us to defend the rights of the poor and needy (Proverbs 31:20). This takes courage. This requires daily, thoughtful interaction. To live independently is a foolish, destructive, and cowardly way of life. What takes more courage after all—self-absorption or self-sacrifice?

To be fearlessly feminine means to turn from the idol of self-centeredness. It means learning to make decisions based on what is best for those we love, rather than what is most convenient or satisfying to us. The cultural cult of convenience is opposed to fearless femininity. When Jesus calls us to leave the god of the mirror and follow His pathway, He is asking us to give over to Him the fear of losing ourselves (Matthew 10:38–39). In the end, the fear of losing ourselves can simply become an excuse for never giving away any of ourselves. What are we afraid of? Do we think that God might be mistaken when He calls us to serve?

Elisabeth Elliot speaks to this point in *Let Me Be a Woman*:

God has set no traps for us. Quite the contrary. He has summoned us to the only true and full freedom. The woman who defines her liberation as doing what she wants, or not doing what she doesn't want, is, in the first place, evading responsibility. Evasion of responsibility is the mark of immaturity. The Woman's Liberation Movement is characterized, it appears, by this very immaturity. While telling themselves that they've come a long way, that they are actually coming of age, they have retreated to a partial humanity, one which refuses to acknowledge the vast significance of the sexual differentiation. (I do not say that they always ignore sexual differentiation itself, but that the *significance* of it escapes

them entirely.) And the woman who ignores that fundamental truth ironically misses the very thing she has set
out to find. By refusing to fulfill the whole vocation of
womanhood she settles for a caricature, a pseudo-
personhood.[8]

Feminism has called us into unnecessary unhappiness,
where we become entwined in the popular hysteria over our
rights as women. We're continually checking our feelings to see
if we're happy. This is not progress. This is following "the stubborn inclinations of their evil hearts." God calls this going
"backward" (Jeremiah 7:22–24). Our happiness is God's concern. Will we trust and obey our heavenly Father? The fearlessly feminine woman learns to abandon the tyranny of self
and bow in humble submission before her Creator and verbalize to Him, just as Mary did two thousand years ago, "I am the
Lord's servant. May it be to me as you have said" (Luke 1:38).

God Honors Fearless Femininity

Think of a woman you admire, someone who consistently lives
out fearless femininity. Is she, as some feminists would have us
believe, repressed and dispirited? Is she a victim of male domi-
nance and a patriarchal society? Are her moral values something to laugh at? Or is she one of the most fulfilled women
you know? Is her life of service one to be emulated?

My friend Helen calls herself a recovering workaholic.
Work used to be her security. Early on in her first marriage her
husband left her. She remained single until she was forty-five,
when she married a wonderful Christian man.

Helen reported to an upper level manager in a major

Fortune 500 company. She led strategic planning, quality improvement, and process analysis initiatives and had several people reporting to her. But, she told me, the higher up she went, the less she liked what she saw. The workplace had a very definite, purposeful plan to shape her into someone—and that someone had to be aggressively unfeminine.

She began to struggle with an inner conflict. She learned quickly that she could not be aggressive and hard-nosed at work without bringing at least some of that home with her. Her husband graciously called it being in "manager mode." But she also saw that if she did not harden herself somewhat, she came home beaten up emotionally by the constant self-promotion and conflict at the office. The wonderful sensitive nature that God had given her as a woman had turned into a *liability* in the workplace.

She looked for a mentor, but could find no one she considered successful who had not given up something of her femininity in the process. Self-esteem was what the marketplace promised, but she had to surrender the beauty of her womanhood to gain it. She decided that was too high a price. So she left her prestigious job and became a full-time homemaker and wife. She has told me that she's glad to be out of the lion's den. She misses the people, but she has no desire to go back into that environment.

She enjoys her marriage more now. She has time to serve her husband so that he can be more productive. She also has time to enjoy her home and time to serve in other ways the Lord opens up. Their marriage is now, as she termed it, "a love affair rather than a business partnership." God, by the way, wastes nothing in our lives. She now uses those same skills she learned in the business world to lead women's ministries in her local church.

Some of you may feel the same conflicts that Helen did and yet cannot leave the marketplace. You may have no choice but to work, perhaps in a tough environment. I've been there, too. I know what you're going through. God is able to guard your heart from the hardening power at work there. But you must set your face with that much greater determination on the ways of God and not be intimidated into a distortion of the woman God made you to be. Pray for great faith and discernment, and God will meet you and encourage you.

These are dangerous days for Christian women. In the name of tolerance we have allowed ourselves to be misled and deluded. We have watched the bird of popular culture flit around the sanctuary of our own homes, thinking that it would eventually fly out on its own, when we should have been chasing it out. We have wasted time and energy sipping from the sewage of this world. We have allowed feminist ideology to triumph in the communications and entertainment industry and ultimately in our homes. How has such a damaging ethos become so popular? Robert Bork writes:

> Popular culture remains just that, popular. The American public watches, listens to, and makes popular art forms it agrees are debased. That is an important point. The entertainment industry is not forcing depravity on an unwilling American public. The demand for decadence is there.[9]

Are we part of that demand? Have we sought the applause of this sin-sickened world as we minimize our own daily responsibilities to those we love? Have we salivated over the things that money and power can buy at the expense of our homes and families? Have we forgotten that "What is highly valued among men is detestable in God's sight" (Luke 16:15)?

I am calling us to exult in our God-given femininity. We must welcome His Word and His ways in our lives. We must stop trying to bring to God our version of what a woman should be, as if He didn't consider our generation and culture when He penned His eternal message to us. I want to help nurture in us a new joy in being what only we can be—godly women, godly wives, godly mothers. I want to help us reclaim territory we have yielded to the feminist movement as we have watched it flit around us. Let's stop playing with popular culture and, by God's grace, fearlessly embrace all that He honors in a woman.

Study Questions

1. Read James 4:4. In what ways do we desire friendship with the world? How do these alliances show hatred toward God?

2. Describe the differences and similarities between your life as a woman now and the lives of your mother and grandmothers.

3. If you work full-time outside your home, why do you do so? How can you manage your situation to be the most honoring to God and those you love?

4. How have you contributed to the demand for decadence in our society? Read Psalm 101:2–3. What objectionable materials do you set before your eyes? What can you do about it?

5. As a daughter, mother, grandmother, sister, niece, friend, how have you been conforming to the patterns of popular culture? Study Romans 12:1–2. Write out a prayer to God telling Him how you plan to offer yourself to Him as a living sacrifice.

Some people, eager for money, have wandered from the faith and pierced themselves with many griefs.

1 TIMOTHY 6:10

No Mistake of God's
FANNIE CROSBY
(1820–1915)

Fannie Jane Crosby has been called "the most important writer of gospel hymn texts in American history."[1] She was blinded as a tiny infant through improper medical care, but she never revealed bitterness or depression because of her disability. She attended and taught at the New York School for the Blind, where she met her husband, Alexander Van Alstyne.

Fannie wasn't strong in braille, so she relied on her phenomenal memory to compose and edit poems in her mind. Then she would dictate them. Her nearly nine thousand hymn texts, rich expressions of her faith and hope, have had worldwide influence. She traveled extensively as a speaker in her later years, almost always alone, and witnessed at both rescue missions and at the White House. Although she was the social guest of six presidents, and her poetry was admired by many famous people, she deliberately lived simply. She accepted only about two dollars for each of her compositions.

Fannie began writing gospel texts in her midforties. Her hymns are some of the best loved and most familiar of all time. Heaven and the Lord's return were her favorite subjects. Her titles include "Jesus, Keep Me near the Cross," "All the Way My Savior Leads Me," "Blessed Assurance," "He Hideth My Soul," "To God Be the Glory," and what she referred to as her *heart song,* "Saved by Grace."

God gave her triumph over her life of blindness. She anticipated heaven, where the first sight she would ever see would be the face of her dear Savior as He opened heaven's gates for her and welcomed her home. She wrote in one of her two autobiographies: "If perfect earthly sight were offered to me tomorrow, I would not accept it. Although it may have been a blunder on the physician's part, it was no mistake of God's. I verily believe it was His intention that I should live my days in physical darkness, so as to be better prepared to sing His praises and incite others to do so. I could not have written thousands of hymns—many of which, if you will pardon me for repeating it, are sung all over the world—if I had been hindered by the distractions of seeing all the interesting and beautiful objects that would have been presented to my notice."[2]

CHAPTER THREE

Mired in Materialism

⁂

D o you ever struggle with "If only...?" I do. We lived in the northeast corner of Scotland for four years while my husband worked on his doctorate at the University of Aberdeen, and for three of those years we didn't have a car. When the weather turned blustery or wet (which was much too frequent for my liking), I'd find myself thinking, *"If only* I had a car to carry all these groceries home, my attitude would be much better."

A few years later we were back in the States planting a Presbyterian church in Oregon. Through the gracious gift of our parents we *did* have a car. But somehow, as our boys started growing into their six-foot frames, I couldn't keep my resolve to be content with just any car. I thought, *"If only* I had a bigger car, I know I would be happy then." I tried to keep myself in check by not longing for a full conversion van—a minivan would do!

Eventually we did get a minivan, and I truly was happy. At least I was happy until a ministry change for Ray and a move to the northern suburbs of Chicago necessitated my going to work. We tried to be patient as every morning and evening Ray got each one of us where we were supposed to be and back again. Ray was more successful at this patience thing than I, and as the years passed and our family's activities and responsibilities expanded, that old longing crept into my thought patterns again: *"If only* we had *two* cars, I could be so much more efficient. It's just too hard to juggle all of life's details for the six of us with only one car. It wouldn't have to be a luxury vehicle. Just something to get around in. Then I would really, truly be happy."

As you are no doubt expecting, eventually we were able to get a second car, and it did help relieve some of the stress of work schedules and appointments and sports events and church activities. And I truly did find it easier to be happy. But then as the months rolled by, my discontentment shifted from our car situation to our home. How shabby our furniture looked! Soon I found myself thinking, "If only…"

Frustrated Daydreams or Contented Reality?

Can you identify at all? It may not be a car that makes you struggle with "If only…" Perhaps it's a nicer house or more money to decorate the house you're in or a family vacation or a computer or a new wardrobe or things (even good things) for the children like money for the eye doctor or the orthodontist or soccer shoes. So we spend our years living in frustrated daydreams rather than in contented reality.

The world we live in helps us build those daydreams. We are bombarded with signals that tell us we will finally be happy when we have everything we want—that happiness can be found in things. So we browse through the malls and the catalogs and the car dealerships searching for that perfect something that will satisfy the restlessness niggling at our hearts. I heard recently that Americans on the average spend 5–15 percent more money than they make. No wonder finances are a leading source of stress in many families.

As women, we long to make our homes a haven, our gardens inviting, and our meals enticing. We want to clothe our children adequately and provide them with a solid education. We desire to create family memories, whether they center around a gameboard or a well-planned vacation. And we often feel that our budget restricts our creative intentions. When it does, we often respond in fear. We fear our dreams will never be realized, our children will be deprived, and our memories will be soured.

There is also the struggle, even for Christians, of viewing the lifestyles of our friends and others in the church with envy. We look at their homes, their wardrobes, their jewelry, their vacations, and somehow we feel that we don't quite fit the pattern. So we withdraw and withhold ourselves from entering into true Christian fellowship. This is Satan's trap. He loves to divide us with unnecessary barriers and keep us spinning our wheels and concentrating more on the external than the internal.

Let's free ourselves from the fear of the feminine ideal. Let's be women who put aside our petty insecurities and love each other deeply—deeply enough to live above our fears and jealousies and self-centeredness. Then we'll have sincere, real, comforting relationships that can absorb the inevitable differences that the body of Christ contains.

Are you under financial stress? Do you struggle with "If only..."? Are you nagged by fears that you will never really have what you think you need? Do you withhold yourself from others because of embarrassment over your financial situation?

Are you bogged down in the mire of materialism? Here are three principles to help you resist its powerful pull.

Learn to look at possessions the way God does.

The Bible speaks a lot about money and material possessions. Jesus said more about money than He did about prayer. In fact, thirteen of His thirty-eight parables address material possessions. Obviously, how we handle our belongings is important to Christ.

First Timothy 6 issues a potent warning about money. In this letter to his son in the faith, Paul warns against false teaching, and he charges Timothy to live in faithfulness to God, especially in the area of financial matters. Paul helps us look at our possessions from God's point of view: "For we brought nothing into the world, and we can take nothing out of it" (1 Timothy 6:7). Material resources are equally irrelevant at our entrance to and exit from this present world. Birth and death mark the parentheses of our short earthly existence. Possessions are for this world *only*. Material things can *only* belong to a material world.

In light of eternity, the things we covet here have absolutely no permanence. What can we take out of this world? Nothing but our eternal souls. Let us be women who cultivate the internal more than the external, who judge earthly possessions for what they truly are—only temporal. They are pleasing to be sure, but those pleasures can turn into a vicious trap of self-centeredness when temporal things become too important or necessary. The fearlessly feminine woman lives with eternity's mark on her innermost being.

THE CORROSIVE EFFECTS OF MATERIALISM

First Timothy 6:9 warns us that materialism ruins us. It corrodes and destroys our souls: "People who want to get rich fall into temptation and a trap and into many foolish and harmful desires that plunge men into ruin and destruction." As we set our desires upon the acquisition of wealth, we stumble suddenly and unexpectedly into sin. Our passions snare us, and almost without knowing it we become envious, insecure, stingy, withdrawn, intimidated, self-centered.

Notice the word *want* in this verse. The mere *desire* to get rich destroys people. It sets us on a course that is harmful to all we hold dear. Our moral sense becomes blurred as we allow this desire to absorb us, and we find ourselves sinking, submerged, almost drowning in harmful and destructive patterns of thinking and living. How many homes have suffered because of women who were driven by the desire for *more?* How many children have missed valuable years under a mother's care because she wanted to supply them with more *things?*

THE PAINFUL EFFECTS OF MATERIALISM

Paul warns that the adoration of material things leads to all kinds of evil and can even lead to wandering from the faith: "For the love of money is a root of all kinds of evil. Some people, eager for money, have wandered from the faith and pierced themselves with many griefs" (1 Timothy 6:10). We can be led astray so easily in this area, not rejecting the Lord in the strictest sense, but living lives that are out of accord with the spirit of contentment that should temper our hearts at all times.

When money is desired, wanted, strongly yearned for, it

holds a certain power over us. We become restless and begin to worship at the altar of self-gratification. Does this really satisfy? Could it ever? Paul warns us that it brings only pain—self-inflicted pain.

The Controlling Effects of Materialism

We pour a lot of emotional energy into that which we esteem and cherish. In Matthew 6:19–24, Jesus taught that what we value captures our hearts and controls us. The love of money can cloud our judgment and shackle our resolve to serve God with all our heart and soul and mind. It can trip us up and drain us of our joy and inner calm and leave in its wake anxiety, jealousy, and all sorts of turmoil. These longings and daydreams exhaust our emotional resources and offend our Creator.

Jesus warned that money can master us and deaden our devotion to God. You cannot give both God and possessions equal place in your heart. One must be your master. So which one do you serve? Which one do you treasure and value? What do you daydream about? To what do you devote your time and energy? If you're not sure, look at your checkbook and calendar for the past few months. "For where your treasure is, there your heart will be also" (Matthew 6:21). Where is your treasure? Where is your heart?

While we were living in Scotland, my husband's parents stopped to visit us on their way home from ministering in India. Their work had been demanding, but fruitful, and now they had come to spend some time with the six of us. We sat visiting, catching up on the many months of separation and enjoying each other's company.

When it was time for dinner, Daddy said to Mother, "Anne,

why don't we call the airport and see if there's any sign of your ring?" It was then I noticed something was missing. For years I had seen Mother wear a beautiful jewel-studded ring on her right hand, a generous thank-you from a neighbor she had led to the Lord. As Daddy called the airport, Mother told us she had removed her ring to put on hand lotion while they were waiting for their connection in London several hours before. She was so tired she forgot to put it back on, and it must have fallen to the floor unnoticed when she stood up to get on their flight. The ring—valuable in itself and priceless as a personal gift—was surely lost. And yet that wasn't foremost on her mind as we welcomed her into our home.

I asked her how she could be so calm about what seemed to me a real loss.

"Well, Jani," she said, "I have to think the right thing in my head. Yes, I am sad to lose my ring because it was very precious to me, but it was only a thing. If I lose everything, I still have all the riches of Christ."

Mother demonstrated unmistakable allegiance to God, not mammon, as her emotional Master. Whom do you serve?

Learn to be content.

Have you ever known someone who was peaceful and at rest with life and its challenges, someone who never complained or whined or cast doubt on the Lord's goodness? Contentment is rare these days. It has always been. Ray has a book titled *The Rare Jewel of Christian Contentment,* by Jeremiah Burroughs. It was published in 1648, but it could use a good dusting off for today's Christian.

CLOSENESS TO GOD FEEDS CONTENTMENT

Paul tells us in 1 Timothy 6:6 that "godliness with contentment is great gain." What do we gain? We gain a sense of calmness, quietude, a certain independence from our circumstances that will guard our hearts from coveting anything more or anything else. Contentment allows us to abandon *our* will and cheerfully embrace *God's* will. Contentment means that our emotions are not ruled by our environment. We gain peace of mind no matter what our circumstances (Philippians 4:11–13). Personal communion with God is the garden in which godliness with contentment grows because God is so worth having. As it sprouts, we learn more and more how to abandon our own will and embrace our Father's. And that is *great gain.*

Contentment opens up for us the experience of Hebrews 13:5: "Keep your lives free from the love of money and be content with what you have, because God has said, 'Never will I leave you; never will I forsake you.'" God's presence is enough. No more nail biting, no more chafing, no more restless nights. You see, our real need is not more things, but God himself. The solution to our grumbling discontent is not raising the quality of our lives to a certain level. We will only know true contentment when our heart can say with the psalmist, "Whom have I in heaven but you? And earth has nothing I desire besides you" (Psalm 73:25). Why is contentment gain? What makes it rich? It draws us ever closer to God in peace and rest and faith.

Of course, we are earthly beings, and by God's design we do have material needs. But what level of provision should we consider adequate? First Timothy 6:8 says, "But if we have food and clothing, we will be content with that." It is remarkable that the list is so short—no minivan, no summer holiday, no condo at the beach!

My problem is trying to determine *how much* food and covering. Of course I could be content if I had *her* wardrobe and *her* food budget! It comes back again and again to God's will for *me*. God calls us to be content with our food and clothing for today, and Jesus told us not to worry about these things for tomorrow (Matthew 6:34). Do you have something to wear today? All right, it may not be what you want to wear, but you do have something? Did you have something to eat at your last meal? Then, stop worrying and learn contentment.

It was November 1984, and we had been in Scotland for over three years. We were struggling financially, and I was beginning to complain. Thanksgiving was approaching, and we had no money for a turkey dinner. I don't know why it was such a big deal to me. Thanksgiving isn't even celebrated in the U.K.! But it seemed important to keep our family traditions alive, and I was ready for a feast. I found myself grumbling and pouting throughout that week and even through Thanksgiving Day. I was anything but thankful for the small amount of ground beef I made into a homemade pizza that night for dinner. My anxiety and resentment ate away every bit of contentment in my soul.

The next morning I was watching TV while I nursed our little Gavin. The BBC was breaking the news story of the widespread famine in Ethiopia. I watched with growing horror the tragic images of suffering mothers and children lying along dirt paths, starving to death. As Eric, Krista, and Dane rushed in the door for lunch (in Scotland the kids were given time to come home for the noon meal) and sat down to their peanut butter sandwiches and milk, I found myself convicted and humbled. I had food for my little ones. My picky, complaining spirit was sin. Through my tears we prayed over lunch that

Friday, and I asked God to give me a heart that says, "But if we have food and clothing, we will be content with that."

Materialism is a " black hole," always leaving us looking for more. I once heard that when multimillionaire J. Paul Getty was asked how much money it would take to make him happy, his reply was, "Just a little more." Do you feel this way?

STRONG ACTION FORTIFIES CONTENTMENT

How can we learn a spirit of contentment that frees us to help meet the needs of those around us and fully enjoy all that God has given us? Paul's advice to Timothy will help us.

> But you, man of God, flee from all this, and pursue righteousness, godliness, faith, love, endurance and gentleness. Fight the good fight of the faith. Take hold of the eternal life to which you were called when you made your good confession in the presence of many witnesses. (1 Timothy 6:11–12)

Notice the four strong verbs: *flee, pursue, fight,* and *take hold.* Contentment is not some neutral state of mind. We're told to *flee* from "all this"—shun, run from, refuse to stand around debating with temptation. Shun the desire to get rich, flee from the love of money, refuse to stand around and debate with your grasping, greedy heart.

We're further challenged to *pursue*—set our hearts upon, aim at upright conduct toward—both God and man. We're admonished to pursue:

- righteousness—learning to care more about doing right than acquiring things;

- godliness—showing what God is like to those around us;
- faith—developing an ever deepening trust in our heavenly Father rather than our circumstances;
- love—striving to live out 1 Corinthians 13 in all our relationships;
- endurance—becoming women who are willing to cheerfully tough it out;
- gentleness—leaving no room for a strident, competitive, defensive spirit.

Paul goes on to call us to "fight the good fight," doing battle with anything that would cross swords with our faith. We must *take hold*—internalize, personalize—our own call to faith in Christ Jesus. We must learn to resist the foolish traps of materialism as we take hold of the eternal life to which we are called. We must loosen our grasp on the fleeting pleasures of earth which rot and rust and leave us agitated in our souls. Those snares and temptations are the enemies of fearless femininity. They suck our souls dry of peace and contentment.

FINANCIAL BROODING

Maybe you're thinking, "Jani, I'm not worried about the big things like cars and furniture. I would hardly call my needs fleeting pleasures. I just want to have enough milk and bread to feed my family until the next paycheck arrives. The children's shoes are too small, and my glasses have broken beyond repair. Where will the money come from?"

Jesus tells us to come to God with our worries. He says:

Therefore I tell you, do not worry about your life, what you will eat or drink; or about your body, what you will wear. Is not life more important than food, and the body more important than clothes? Look at the birds of the air; they do not sow or reap or store away in barns, and yet your heavenly Father feeds them. Are you not much more valuable than they? (Matthew 6:25–34)

Your Father values you deeply. Don't fuss over your earthly needs as if you didn't belong to the one who feeds the birds of the air and clothes the lilies of the field. Remember that He has placed you deeply in His heart. Trust in His fatherly protection and loving care. You are free to go about God's business today and leave tomorrow with Him. Your heavenly Father "knows that you need them" (v. 32).

Worry eats at us. It mires our hearts in apprehension and fear. It saps our strength and drains our cheer. Is it possible to be in financial need and yet be dignified and cheerful? Yes! We must not give in to the myth that an uncertain financial future is an unbearable state of affairs. The people to whom Jesus was speaking had no IRAs or bank statements to calm their fears about the future. They had no safety net to fall back on. And yet Jesus looks them right in the eye and calls them to a worry-free faith. Why? Because a Father who takes such excellent care of His birds and flowers will surely provide His children with all they need.

Imagine my going into my child's room to kiss him good-night only to find him crying fitfully into his pillow. When I question him, he tells me that he's afraid he'll be thirsty tomorrow. I almost laugh at his worry, but instead I calmly assure him that if I water our houseplants—silly houseplants that sometimes die after only a few months—then of course I will make sure that my precious, darling, beloved child has enough water to drink. A loving parent delights in providing for his child. Even so, our heavenly Father knows our needs, and He will take care of them according to His good and wise will. We can find our contentment in Him.

I don't know your personal situation right now. You may be a young college graduate, faced with enormous school loans to pay off; a single mother, trying to feed her children; a stay-at-home mom, cutting many corners in order to make it on her husband's income; a missionary who has just learned that a contributor has decided to stop supporting her; or a retired lady who is finding that her expenses exceed her means. But wherever we are, let's be fearless, not because we are oblivious to reality, but because we are related to True Reality. Our loving Father calls us to leave our financial brooding and settle down with child-like trust in Him. One of my favorite hymns says it this way:

> *Only be still and wait His leisure*
> *In cheerful hope, with heart content*
> *To take whate'er thy Father's pleasure*
> *And all-discerning love have sent;*
> *Nor doubt our inmost wants are known*
> *To Him who chose us for His own.*
> GEORG NEUMARK, 1621–1681

Learn to lay up treasures for eternity.

Our final principle concerns giving. How might you expect this verse to be completed: "Command those who are rich in this present world to _____"? Wouldn't it be easy if we had a formula to follow, something like: "Command those who are rich in this present world to give 23 percent to their local churches, 12 percent to missionaries, 10 percent to parachurch organizations, 5 percent to local charities, and then live on the rest"? But the Holy Spirit doesn't give us an itemized budget to follow, no easy formula to soothe our consciences each month as we write our checks. Instead He speaks to our hearts:

> Command those who are rich in this present world not to be arrogant nor to put their hope in wealth, which is so uncertain, but to put their hope in God, who richly provides us with everything for our enjoyment. Command them to do good, to be rich in good deeds, and to be generous and willing to share. In this way they will lay up treasure for themselves as a firm foundation for the coming age, so that they may take hold of the life that is truly life. (1 Timothy 6:17–19)

Genuine Wealth

The Bible tells us not to become arrogant or haughty. We must never think, "Aren't I clever to have done so well?" Our security and hope must never depend on our ability to control events or correct needy situations because of our financial status. Rather, we are to put our "hope in God, who richly provides us with everything for our enjoyment." It is interesting that God provides these things "for our enjoyment." We are to trust in God and then totally enjoy what we have—enjoy, but hold lightly.

Along with a humble enjoyment of all God has provided for us, He commands us to be "rich in good deeds." This kind of wealth can't be deposited in the bank, but it is the measure of true wealth. Our willingness to serve, our availability, our compassion when we see needs, our responsiveness to those who naturally irritate us, our openness to inconvenience, our flexibility in the midst of pressing schedules, these are the gauges of genuine wealth.

INVEST IN ETERNITY

When we practice 1 Timothy 6:18, we transfer the wealth of this present world into a "firm foundation for the coming age." The parable of the rich fool warns us to be on our guard against greed (Luke 12:13–21). We are to be rich toward God. When our hearts are turned toward Him we can be "rich in good deeds...generous and willing to share." Then our possessions will hold no ultimate power over us. We will be free to enjoy—yes, truly enjoy—what we have, but not hold it so tightly that it controls us. Our hearts won't be dominated by the stock market or new tax laws or comparisons with others. We will live with eternity in view, building for a confident future on an unshakable foundation.

Our passage calls us to "take hold of the life that is truly life" (1 Timothy 6:19). The love of money can rob us of true life. Our possessions become our security, and then we put our hope in our uncertain wealth, rather than God. Proverbs 23:4–5 says, "Do not wear yourself out to get rich; have the wisdom to show restraint. Cast but a glance at riches, and they are gone, for they will surely sprout wings and fly off to the sky like an eagle."

Our efforts here on earth will ultimately rise toward the skies—either into the unknown or straight toward heaven. Our earthly possessions and riches will one day sprout wings and fly off "to the sky like an eagle"—either through the inevitable decay of day-to-day existence, or through our own death. But 1

Timothy 6:18 tells us there are certain things we can do here on earth that will fly straight up to heaven: "Command them to do good, to be rich in good deeds, and to be generous and willing to share." Our good deeds, our generosity, our willingness to share will precede us into eternity as treasures laid up by women who know the value of true wealth.

GIVE ALL THAT YOU CAN

We can never give too much. Think of the scene in the temple when the poor widow gave everything she had (Luke 21:1–2). Jesus could have cautioned her to take back one of her coins, and still she would have been giving 50 percent. Instead, He commended her generous spirit and then entrusted her to His Father's care. He knew she was safe there. And so are we.

My parents have shown me what this looks like in real life. My mother and father worked hard in their early years to enable Dad to complete his education. With four young children to support, this entailed tiring, menial jobs and late nights. Dad traveled all week throughout the early years of their marriage and also gave one weekend a month to duty in the Naval Reserve.

Mother worked hard at home to keep the house running smoothly on a tight budget. I remember her teaching me how to plan our meals so the six of us could eat on thirty dollars per week. I also know that all through those years they sacrificed in order to save for our future.

As I grew up, I became aware of their remarkable generosity to the cause of Christ. They had no problem and still don't, cheerfully sharing their hard-earned savings with worthy individuals and causes. They have given away cars, furniture, stocks and bonds in order to further Christ's kingdom. They are "rich in good deeds," laying up "treasure for themselves as a firm foundation" and thus taking "hold of the life that is truly life."

We must be women who are rich toward God, who hope in Him, who give all that we can, who are willing to fight the battle for that which is truly life, who store treasures in heaven rather than here on earth. We must fearlessly prepare for the coming age on a firm foundation of generosity and acts of kindness. Let's get over the habit of thinking "If only...". Let's lay aside our worries by trusting in our loving Father's care. As He lifts us from the mire of materialism, let's offer to Him our hearts—hearts that are fearlessly feminine.

Study Questions

1. What "If only..." are you struggling with? What would it take to make you truly at peace with your financial situation?

2. By what/whom is your heart held captive? What do you treasure most in this world? Survey your calendar and checkbook. Now read Matthew 6:19–24. Write out a response to what God is teaching you.

3. What is robbing you of contentment right now? Why do you think God has you in this particular situation?

4. What do Luke 6:38 and 2 Corinthians 9:6–8 teach us about generosity?

5. What deeds of kindness is God calling you to initiate?

A wife of noble character who can find?
She is worth far more than rubies.

PROVERBS 31:10

What More Could a Guy Ask For?
RUTH BELL GRAHAM
(1920–)

R uth Bell Graham has modeled for today's women how to live with one of the world's most famous men. Married to Billy Graham since 1943, she has lived out her commitment to serve Jesus Christ, her husband, and her family with uncompromising dedication. Her family and friends know her as a woman of depth, vitality, and joy. Her daughter has written, "I now understand that her joy did not stem from perfect or ideal circumstances, but from a deep, abiding love affair with the Lord Jesus."[1]

Born in China to medical missionary parents, she spent the first seventeen years of her life in Asia. She met her husband while she was a student at Wheaton College in Illinois. He tells it like this:

> I straightened up, and there she was. Standing there, looking right at me, was a slender, hazel-eyed movie starlet! I said something polite, but I was flustered and embarrassed. It took me a month to muster the courage to ask her out for a date.... If I had not been smitten with love at the first sight of Ruth Bell, I would certainly have been the exception. Many of the men at Wheaton thought she was stunning. Petite, vivacious, smart, talented, witty, stylish, amiable, and unattached. What more could a guy ask for?[2]

Her marriage to a world famous evangelist has been a series of good-byes. As their five children started arriving, she became what many ministry wives come to be—the mom in the middle. Caught between the needs of her traveling husband and the demands of her growing family, she expressed her heart and her prayers in writing.

The world was watching for any flaws and expecting perfection. The attention, naturally, was hard for Ruth. She said it made her feel like a beetle under a stone as the stone was removed. She wrote, "And behind it all, lurking in the background, is that fear that somewhere in this avalanche of publicity we will stumble and disgrace Him.... It's silly to bewail this publicity. It may be a cross. It may be an opportunity. It may be both. Our hearts' deepest desire is that in it all, *He* may be glorified and accomplish His purpose."[3]

Through it all—a husband who was often far away, the searching spotlight of fame, the heartache of children wandering from their Christian heritage before settling in deeply with Jesus—through it all, she has remained a joyful servant of her Lord. What is her secret? It is her courageous commitment to Jesus Christ, her deep loyalty to her husband and their marriage, and a zealous desire to see God's purpose for them together fulfilled through their ministry.

CHAPTER FOUR

The Fearlessly Feminine Wife

No one intends to end up in a mediocre marriage, and yet look around you. We live in a day of impoverished marriages: weak in purpose, depleted of vitality, deprived of real romance, and confused about the scriptural obligations of sustained fidelity. What do you want most from your marriage? What would make it deeply satisfying? As you face the years ahead, what are your greatest fears?

As Ray and I have counseled young people, we have been taken aback by their almost paralyzing fears about marriage. They fear the absolute openness and vulnerability that an authentic marriage requires. They fear the pain of exposure that a one-flesh relationship inevitably brings. They fear failure as they sense their own inadequacies and see other marriages crumbling around them. They wonder if they can really live by their vows. What is a promise worth? They see that the costly commitments inherent in a lifelong relationship will limit them. They fear that their marriage might become a trap.

Their questions are not trivial. Marriage should never be entered into lightly. The courage to live by our creeds, the willingness to be genuine and intimate with another human being, and the discipline of submission to a lifelong commitment are sobering prospects indeed!

It is not, however, the institution of marriage that is to be feared. The problem is not the nature of marriage. The problem is us. We are at fault. Marriage only unmasks our inadequacies. Marriage is not our enemy. It is a part of God's perfect, pre-Fall creation. Hebrews 13:4 says, "Marriage should be honored by all." When we women honor our marriages with fearless femininity, what sweet compensations follow. As we yield to God's design for marriage, we are stretched in liberating ways that free us to receive sincere love, real romance, and tangible security.

Wouldn't you relish the chance to be caught up in an extended, authentic, unbroken love affair? You and I take a huge step toward realizing that goal when we bring to our marriage a fearlessly feminine wife. Let me suggest four principles to help us in this pursuit.

Live above Your Feelings

It was September of 1981, and we had just moved to the northeast corner of Scotland for Ray to begin his doctoral work at the University of Aberdeen. One Saturday found us at the Highland Games at Braemar, which were always attended by members of the royal family who spent their annual holiday at nearby Balmoral Castle. Diana and Charles had been married just a few weeks, and they attended the games that day. Although we found the dancing and piping competitions entertaining and the caber tossing impressive, I myself was preoccupied with the newlyweds. I was particularly thrilled to get a curbside wave as they drove past after the games were finished. Was ever a marriage wished so much happiness? Yet within a few short years, we watched sadly as their fairy tale romance disintegrated, leaving many to wonder what it takes to make a marriage last. If a prince and princess can't find happiness, who can?

What, after all, is marital love? What is it worth? As Christian women we must rise above the belief that warm, loving feelings are what make a good marriage and keep it strong. Marriage is more than a mere alliance between two people who love each other. It is a binding commitment made before God and witnesses that goes beyond feelings. It is a commitment not only to a husband, *but to the marriage itself*. It is a devotion to the objective truths of Scripture that teach us of its one-flesh mystery (Ephesians 5:31–33) and of how God hates divorce (Malachi 2:16). It is a promise that says I will act in a loving way toward my husband even when the feelings aren't there, because my marriage is more important than my feelings. Feelings are so undependable. They cave in at the least disappointment, like a house of cards jarred by the slightest tremor.

How many wedding ceremonies have you attended where 1 Corinthians 13 has been read, as it was at Charles and Diana's wedding? We intuitively recognize that the ideals found in that biblical passage could only help lead to marital fulfillment. Let's look at verses 4–7. What do they teach us about living above our feelings?

PATIENCE, KINDNESS, AND HUMILITY

Real love calls us to patience, kindness, and humility. "Love is patient, love is kind. It does not envy, it does not boast, it is not proud" (v. 4). A fearlessly feminine wife can relax with her man. She can laugh at his inevitable foibles, quirks, weaknesses, and eccentricities. And she can allow him the freedom to laugh at hers as well.

Marriage, with all its exposure and intimacies, will bring certain feelings of annoyance and impatience. Are you tired of his need to unwind in front of the TV? Approach him with patience. Talk things through with your husband with kindness and humility. Are you envious of the hours he spends on his hobbies? Join him. Extend yourself to him over and over again. Do you feel put upon because of all that you must bring to make your marriage work? When your good feelings ebb and you're tempted to withdraw, remember God's definition of love. Love is patient and kind, humble and other-oriented. Ask God to use these very difficulties as an occasion to help you rise above your feelings.

KEEP SHORT ACCOUNTS

Real love calls us to keep short accounts with our husbands. "It is not rude, it is not self-seeking, it is not easily angered, it keeps no record of wrongs" (v. 5). There is a certain earthiness to marriage that often relaxes the courtesies we naturally use with those outside our home. The daily routines and pressures of life tempt us to be uptight, rude, and withdrawn with each other. Do you operate on a short fuse? God calls you to rise above your explosive feelings of indignation. Wipe clean the mental list of past hurts you keep harbored in your heart. The fearlessly feminine woman approaches her husband with a graciousness, courtesy, and respect that rises above her mood swings. Ask God to help you avoid unnecessary quarrels that bring discord to your relationship. Keep short accounts with the man you are going to spend the rest of your life with. Offer up to God your frustration over those incurable character traits you had thought would change over time. Live your marriage by faith—faith in the God who called you to this commitment and who has not abandoned you in it. He will help you to honor your marriage with grace and kindness.

PURITY AND HONESTY

Real love calls us to purity and honesty with each other. "Love does not delight in evil but rejoices with the truth" (v. 6). Perhaps your romance has cooled because you have dallied in activities that compromise marital fidelity. Certain entertainments and relationships can throw water on the flame of your feelings for your husband. Avoid them at any cost. Whatever drives a wedge between a man and a wife must be shunned as evil. It threatens true happiness. Take no delight in it. Never do anything alone that you couldn't do with your husband's ready approval. There must be no secrets that might build barriers between you. Can your husband trust you completely? Proverbs 31:11–12 says, "Her husband has full confidence in her and lacks nothing of value. She brings him good, not harm, all the days of her life."

NEVER GIVE UP

Real love never gives up. "It always protects, always trusts, always hopes, always perseveres" (v. 7). There is a loyalty to marital love that is faithful and enduring. This kind of love chooses to bear a husband's burdens cheerfully. Real love lives out a patient confidence and a forward-looking hope that declares, "Our marriage is worth it."

Perhaps you have heard of the responsibilities Dr. Robertson McQuilkin has borne over the past several years. He resigned his post as president of Columbia Bible College and

Seminary in Columbia, South Carolina (now known as Columbia International University) in order to care for his wife full-time. She has Alzheimer's disease. Refusing all self-pity and false heroics, he is proving true to his vow to love his wife "in sickness and in health." He is living out a love that protects and perseveres. If the tables had been turned, his wife doubtless would have done the same for him.

Are you your husband's most ardent defender? Can he count on you to stand by him? Does he see in you the radiant "I believe in you" that every man needs? Protect his reputation. Guard his privacy. Believe the best of him. And always be there for him—always.

Let's trust God enough to hang in there until the romance returns. Our feelings must not dictate our actions, or else emotions become our god. The fearlessly feminine wife trusts God so much that she turns from her fears and obeys God's Word boldly. Let's be women who live by faith, even when the feelings sometimes fade.

But let's *not* be women who settle for less than the best in our relationship with our husbands. The fearlessly feminine woman is a lover. While real love is *more* than a feeling, it is *not* less. God delights in love. He defines Himself in terms of love (1 John 4:8). He is not antifeelings! He lifts up a marital love that is thoroughly captivating and intoxicating (Proverbs 5:18–20). When King Solomon advises his son on marriage, he says a husband should "*rejoice* in the wife of your youth…may her breasts *satisfy* you *always*, may you *ever* be *captivated* by her love" (italics mine). The fearlessly feminine wife brings joy, satisfaction, and a mysteriously captivating love to her marriage.

Lay Aside Your Pride

Self-gratification is easy to condemn in others and easy to defend in myself. If my own life doesn't unfold as I expected it would or should, I may somehow justify leaving the relationship. But marriage demands an inevitable, and valid, loss of my independence as I yield to my husband. This is why marriage is not for the faint of heart. Christian marriage requires that I be fearless. It takes courage to build a great marriage, because the very nature of this union demands surrender, a losing of my life, a giving up of freedoms. Marriage cannot coexist with my sacred autonomy. Marriage imposes arduous, humbling, bewildering, and sometimes frustrating responsibilities on each partner.

But the courage it takes to lay aside my solitary ego is worth it. This kind of fearless femininity creates a bond that is unique, fulfilling, rich with God's blessing. God calls that relationship becoming one flesh: "And they will become one flesh" (Genesis 2:24). What does it mean to become "one flesh"? Recently my own dear Ray preached:

> Marriage fuses one man with one woman in one fully shared life experience. "One flesh" means more than sexual union. Sex seals and symbolizes and refreshes the one-flesh relationship, but a marriage is more than legalized sexual intimacy. It is the lifelong bonding of one man with one woman in one life fully shared. We must belong fully and belong only to each other. A one-flesh relationship builds a union with no barriers between, but a strong barrier around.

Some of us fear those barriers. We may think, "If I construct a marriage with no barriers between and a solid barrier around, I could become entrapped." Now it is true that marriage is a trap of sorts. To become one flesh—not just one body in our sexual union, but one flesh in all of life—requires a commitment that *does* seal us to each other. But let's not fear this bond. We will give our hearts to *something* in marriage— either a joyful, exhilarating, satisfying, God-pleasing marriage, or the loneliness of our own self-centeredness even within the bonds of marriage. If, in fear, we choose self-protection over the surrender that a one-flesh relationship asks of us, we will miss out on real happiness.

Think for a moment of those whose marriages inspire and delight you. Don't you always think of them as a unit? Jerry and Jeanne, Ray and Anne, David and Carolyn—two people belonging fully and only to each other. True fulfillment in our marriages will come *not* in putting ourselves first, but in a glad self-offering for the sake of the other. We must get through *that* barrier to achieve a one-flesh intimacy. In so doing, we will build a lifelong bond that nothing can penetrate "'til death do us part."

Don't Recoil from God's Call to Submission

No matter how often we hear that submission relates to every part of the body of Christ, it is as wives that our faith is most clearly tested. Submission is a hated and feared word these days. Our culture often portrays it as weakness, codependence, victimization.

But how does God regard submission? He dignifies it as an offering to Himself, which He surely accepts with sweet approval. Look at Ephesians 5:22: "Wives, submit to your husbands *as to the Lord*" (italics mine). To choose deference over defiance, yielding rather than competing, meekness instead of arrogance, flexibility rather than stubbornness—this is kingdom work. To build a God-honoring marriage by putting self-obsession on the cross is a glorious spiritual liberation.

Let's consider how a woman offers submission to her husband. It does *not* mean she must always agree with her husband—that's boring, as well as impossible! In a one-flesh relationship there must be open, honest, and clear communication. But within the bonds of marriage there must also be a certain adaptability in the way a wife relates to her husband. A husband needs a wife who can flex with him, someone who won't fall apart at the least provocation. After she has talked and prayed a problem through, a wife must be willing to accept her husband's legitimate concerns.

Godly submission says, "How can I help you reach your goals and support you as you lead us forward to the glory of God?" Does your husband see in you his greatest helper? Since creation, God has called us as wives to be helpers: "The LORD God said, 'It is not good for the man to be alone. I will make a helper suitable for him'"(Genesis 2:18). What a strong word *helper* is! Think of a partner, a coworker, a supporter, an advocate. This is what we are called to be for our husbands. A helper gives aid and support from a position of strength. God Himself is called a *helper* (Deuteronomy 33:29; Psalm 118:7). Let's not shrink from our calling to help and support our men. God made us "suitable"—fitting, entirely appropriate—for our husbands. What a privilege God has given us.

As we fearlessly follow God's command to submit to our husbands, we show our children and others around us that

God's loving purpose is worthy of our trust. We willingly yield to His sovereign kingship over our lives. He *alone* is worthy of our trust and obedience. Ultimately, a wife's submission doesn't say as much about her view of marriage as it does about her view of God. A woman who has a flexible and submissive attitude through the ups and downs of married life is a woman who trusts God with the whole of her existence as a woman. Let's walk confidently in the light of God's Word, for *there* is real life. Let's leave behind our strident, competitive, self-centered fears and rest joyfully in our God-given calling.

As we live this way, we demonstrate for the world what Paul calls in Ephesians 5:32 "a profound mystery." Listen to what my husband has said about the mystery of marriage:

> A "mystery" in the Bible is not a riddle or a secret, but a revealed truth. A biblical mystery is an insight into reality that no scientist or philosopher could ever have discovered with the tools of human research. It is a truth that God had to reveal for us to see it. It is a truth from heaven, not an invention on earth. Paul explains that marriage is a mystery. Marriage reveals something. Astonishingly, a godly marriage points beyond itself to ultimate reality. It points to Christ and His church in love together.... Our marriages are symbolic of that unseen reality. That ultimate reality is Christ's love for us and our joyful submission to Him. A Christian marriage is a little social platform putting on visible display divine love wedded to joyful human devotion.

What is your marriage displaying to those around you? God created you as a woman for a profound purpose. Rejoice in your femininity. Live a life of cheerful submission and trust. God will be honored, you will be happier, and the world will see the beauty of Christ because of your obedience to God's call.

Become Your Husband's Best Friend

Does the pendulum of emotions swing in your marriage, as it does in most? Do you vacillate between a starry-eyed romance and a desperate fear that you have entered into a commitment that might have been a mistake? In marriage—that most intimate of human connections—we sometimes find ourselves feeling frustrated. We long for a marriage of mutual satisfaction, but somehow it seems out of our reach.

Every marriage needs a fresh breakthrough at times. We need to become friends with our husbands. Not that we won't have other friends, but our husbands ought to be our chief confidants, our most loyal allies, our sweetest companions. So, let's think of our husbands as our best friends and cultivate the friendship. Ecclesiastes 4:9–10 says, "Two are better than one, because they have a good return for their work: If one falls down, his friend can help him up. But pity the man who falls and has no one to help him up!" We all—men and women—need someone to help us at times. If that need isn't met in our marriages, the tragedy is that we may turn to others to fulfill it.

TAKE EACH OTHER'S SIDE

How can you build a deep and safe friendship in your marriage? First of all, don't let anything drive a wedge between you and your husband. Whether it is an overflowing toilet, a strained budget, or a death in the family, use that struggle to take each other's side as friends. We women have a tendency to withdraw when we're struggling. Or am I the only wife who, when asked by a sensitive husband, "What's wrong, honey?" replies with a crisp, "Nothing!"

Resist the temptation to bear it alone. Don't think that withdrawal is safer just because it seems to avoid conflict. Friendships thrive on shared concerns. "Two are better than one"—better than withdrawal into yourself!

TELL HIM WHAT YOU NEED

Second, teach your husband how to comfort you. Teach him how to understand your feelings. A man does not understand a woman by instinct. Tell him what you need. Teach him how to help you when you are hurting. If you are unwilling to do this, there will be at least two consequences in your marriage:

1. Your husband may never learn to understand you. Eventually you will be tempted to turn to other sources of comfort, whether it be your boss or your mother or food or shopping or escapist entertainment. You'll be robbing your husband of the satisfaction of fulfilling one of your deepest needs.

2. Your sons will never see up close a model of friendship in marriage to emulate. Soft words and tender gestures are foreign territory for many men. Let your sons observe some of the ways to comfort a woman by seeing their daddy comfort their mother.

OFFER HIM APPRECIATION AND LOYALTY

Another way to befriend your husband is to offer him your appreciation and loyalty so freely that he doesn't have to ask or wait for it. He needs to hear and feel your approval. Speak well of him to his family and his friends. Praise him in front of his children. What does your family hear from you about your husband? Is he late for dinner again? Does he need to be gone on another business trip? You can have one of two responses: "Poor Daddy—he's working so hard. Let's stop and pray for him." Or "Poor me—I can't believe it's happening again."

As you offer him your appreciation, let others be the ones who try to improve him: his boss, his colleagues, his customers, his family. He may be all too aware of his own shortcomings. He needs a wife who accepts him and loves him for who he is, not only for what she's hoping he'll become. Sara Teasdale put it this way in her poem "Appraisal":

> *Never think she loves him wholly,*
> *Never believe her love is blind,*
> *All his faults are locked securely,*
> *In a closet of her mind.*[4]

Let's speak well of our husbands. Let's offer them the loyalty and appreciation of a deep and lasting friendship. And let's keep those closets of our minds securely locked from public examination.

A RESPONSIVE HEART

Finally, become your husband's best friend by giving him your responsive heart. We more readily embrace those who respond well to us, who listen eagerly and share our dreams. Take an active interest in your husband. Find special ways to honor him. Respect him, admire him, regard him, praise him, love him, consider him, notice him, pay attention to him. Be open to exploring new ideas and needs with him. Learn to listen.

Part of giving your husband a responsive heart is being open to all the joys of your physical relationship. You are your husband's only legitimate sexual partner. Don't be a martyr in bed. Learn to enjoy the secrets shared only between a husband and wife. Spend your lifetime exploring the private pleasures of married love. The ecstasies you experience with your husband will give him deep satisfaction and knit you together in a way that only complete sexual intimacy can. The greatest guard to a man's moral purity is the love, loyalty, and genuine affection of a responsive wife. Don't create a vulnerable spot in your marriage. Don't allow a breach in the barrier of your one-flesh union. Instead, let sexual joy protect the integrity of your marriage.

Be a woman who builds a lifelong friendship with your husband. Teach him how to comfort you. Satisfy his needs for loyalty and approval, for a responsive and open heart, for love and affection.

God loves you so much that He has lavished upon you, through Jesus Christ, the resources you need to be a fearlessly feminine wife. By faith in His goodness, open your heart so wide that He can give you a new beginning—

- patiently living above your feelings;
- joyfully surrendering to the one-flesh bond of marriage;
- cheerfully yielding to God's plan for marital submission;
- loyally uniting with your husband in a lasting friendship;
- freely enjoying the sexual intimacies of a real romance.

The woman who boldly follows God's call and draws strength from His love will set before her generation a living picture of the fearlessly feminine wife.

Study Questions

1. Why did you marry your husband? ("I can't remember" is not an acceptable answer!)

2. With what fears are you struggling in your marriage?

3. In what ways are you operating on feelings rather than faith? Review 1 Corinthians 13:4–7, and record at least one way you would like God to help you reach for this standard of love in your marriage.

4. On a scale of one to ten, rate your experience of the "one-fleshness" of your marriage. Are there any lingering barriers between you and your husband? How can you dismantle them?

5. How is God calling you in your marriage to submit "as unto the Lord"?

6. List your three closest friends. Is your husband on that list? Why or why not? How can you be a better friend to your husband?

It is no sign of weakness to want to be married.
It is normal, and it is good.
The courage comes when you sense God calling you to singleness
(for this chapter of your life) and you accept the call with zeal
and creative planning for His glory.

JOHN PIPER

God's Daily Lovingkindnesses
AUDREY WETHERELL JOHNSON
(1907–1984)

W hat have I come to? Am I to give more to those who already have so much?" Miss Johnson's heart sank when she was asked to teach the Bible to five women who were already well instructed. She was recovering in San Fransisco from her sacrificial years of missionary service in China (1936–1950) when confronted with this request.

Raised by a committed Christian family in Leicester, England, the Bible was key in her conversion. She was deeply committed to its authority and taught it with power. She knew God intimately and let Him, not self, lead her life, even in the worst of all possible conditions.

During the Japanese invasion of China in 1942, Miss Johnson was interned in a prison camp. For two and one-half years, she was forced to live with other prisoners in a hut (a former horse stable) crowded with eighty-nine cots, six open toilets, and two wash basins. Her food was limited to a little rice and a one-inch cube of meat daily. She dropped from 145 to 106 pounds. Yet her primary memory was of "God's daily provisions and lovingkindnesses."[1]

After a brief furlough in England, Miss Johnson returned to China, where she taught at the China Bible Seminary in Shanghai. She had every intention of staying there and training teachers for China's millions, but the communists put her under house arrest for eighteen months. They finally forced her to leave China for good in 1950.

Finding herself in the U.S., she poured out her longing to the Lord and prayed about the invitation to teach these five women. She remembered Jeremiah 45:5: "Should you then seek great things for yourself? Seek them not." She agreed to teach the ladies, and thus began Bible Study Fellowship, an interdenominational worldwide ministry with hundreds of classes studying the Bible in depth.

Miss Johnson's constant aim was the transformation of individual lives through BSF. She believed that God desires to personally impact the life of anyone willing to go it alone with Him, to prayerfully study the Bible for herself, and to do whatever the Holy Spirit taught her. She left a legacy of leadership for Bible Study Fellowship, with an emphasis on disciplined and personal Bible study. She believed that through careful study of the Bible, many people would come to know and love and obey the great God to whom she had committed her life.

CHAPTER FIVE

Fearlessly Single

There are many tests in life. For women, I think one of the hardest ones must be singlehood. I have not had to experience this test yet, but I have enough single friends to know that it is a particularly difficult pathway to walk. Being single can cause a certain tension. Somehow a single person must learn to balance the Biblical example to "be content whatever the circumstances" (Philippians 4:11) with the very real and good desire for enjoying all the pleasures and security of married life.

I believe that marriage is good, something to be sought after and prized. I believe that it is God-ordained and is for our benefit and pleasure. But marriage is not the best thing in life— God Himself is. So how can I encourage those of you who are single to be fearlessly feminine and content with God's good gift of singlehood?

God's Gift for Today

Whether you have never been married, or whether you are single because of divorce or death, Romans 8:28 applies as much to you as to your married friend— "In *all things* God works for the *good* of those who love him, who have been called according to his purpose" (italics mine). So, I do not want to offer you condolences. Neither am I going to devote this chapter to the advantages of singleness. Paul explains them in 1 Corinthians 7.

What I do want to do is encourage you to be fearlessly feminine as you embrace God's gift of singleness to you for today. Yes, the Bible calls singleness a gift (1 Corinthians 7:7). Elisabeth Elliot says of her own experience:

Having now spent more than forty-one years being single, I have learned that it is indeed a gift. Not one I would choose. Not one many women would choose. But we do not choose gifts, remember? We are given them by a divine Giver who knows the end from the beginning, and wants above all else to give us the gift of Himself.[2]

Marriage is good. The Bible says so (Genesis 2:18; Proverbs 18:22), and I believe that with all my heart. But it is only good for those God has called to be married. The question of God's goodness is at the core of all our habitual discontent, whether it is over money or infertility or marriage or health concerns.

I am sometimes tempted to think that if God were really good, He would grant me my heart's desire because, of course, He wants me to be happy. But God is not good because He fulfills *my* desires. He is good because He is fulfilling *His* desires, and His desires are good for you and me. Goodness is His very nature—"You are good, and what you do is good" (Psalm 119:68). If God were not good, He would not be God. And He is the one who sets the definition of what is truly good.

Sometimes it is difficult to accept God's goodness as being truly good because it doesn't feel, look, or taste good to us. We equate goodness with what seems pleasant or satisfying in our immediate experience, and then we end up judging God by how He does or doesn't meet *our* standards. We feel slighted if our ideals for happiness are not met. We become fearful that we'll miss out on experiencing all of life. We begin to resent God and wonder if He is being unfair to us.

But it is impossible for God to shortchange any of His children. In Philippians 2:13 Paul tells us that "it is God who works in you to will and to act according to His good purpose." His purpose for you is good (Psalm 23:1; Psalm 84:11; Romans 8:28, 32; Psalm 37). God will not be less good to you than to any of His other daughters. You are single because right now this is God's best for you. You are single because God is always and forever good to you. If this is true, then it is impossible that anything could be better for you right now than to be single.

Being single is not some sort of punishment. You mustn't think that if you were more spiritual, somehow more satisfied with God alone, then God would bring you a husband. You are not single because your lack of spirituality disqualifies you as good marriage material. Nor are you single because your spiritual maturity says you don't need a husband. You are single because this is God's call for you today. His plan for you is good, and He will never betray you.

We cannot rig God's blessings or earn His favor as we seek answers to what we feel are legitimate needs. God is gracious without charge (Isaiah 55:1). He tenderly cares for His children (Isaiah 40:11). He calls us to still and quiet our souls humbly before Him, for both today and the future (Psalm 131). His ways of wisdom are far above our finite minds (Romans 11:33–36). He is good and He can be trusted. Your singleness is a testing of the reality of your faith in the goodness of God, just as any unfulfilled dream this side of heaven is. Today is God's good gift to you. Open it expectantly and use it with fearless femininity.

The Bindings of Our Lives

Consider Hagar in Genesis 16. *Hagar, you may be thinking, what does she have to teach me?* Exactly. She is not what you would call a famous heroine of the faith. How many women name their daughters Hagar? Hagar is the forgotten one. She was a woman who had no control over her life. It was not of her planning, nor was it because of her sin. She was a servant and was used by Sarah to satisfy her mistress's desire to build a family (Genesis 16:2). And after she had submitted to Sarah's demands and Abraham impregnated her, she was abused (Genesis 16:6). So she ran away.

There is a little bit of Hagar in me, as I imagine there is in you. We long to escape the bindings of our lives. Those bindings don't always revolve around being single. Some women long to escape the confinements of a loveless marriage or a challenging child or financial stress or poor health. But God calls us to peace in the midst of our confinements because we have learned to trust the one who sets our boundaries.

Hagar met God in the desert—in that dry, barren place to which she was fleeing. When He asked her where she had come from, she could tell Him. But when He asked her where she was going, she had no idea. When we run to escape, we are always running *from* something, but rarely know where we are going. We only feel that anything—even a desert—would be better than what we are running from.

God understood Hagar's fear, as He understands yours. God saw where she was. He did not overlook her. She came to know Him as "the God who sees me" (Genesis 16:13). God sees *you* in your *desert* place. He is not overlooking you. He will not forget you. You can trust Him to lead you forward.

The fearlessly feminine woman accepts her singleness as the place in life where she can best experience God. Our identity as women must never be found in our marital status. Our identity must always be anchored in Christ. The fearlessly feminine woman does not perceive herself as one of the "have-nots." She knows she has everything in Christ and a glorious future. "He who did not spare his own Son, but gave him up for us all—how will he not also, along with him, graciously give us all things?" (Romans 8:32).

Discontentment touches everyone, whether single or married. Whether it concerns money or children or relationships or vocation, dissatisfaction springs from the evil in our hearts that puts self on the throne and tries to tell God how to run things. God calls that kind of arrogance idolatry (1 Samuel 15:22–23). Obedience to God knows no limits or conditions. Any day might bring a change in a woman's status, married or single. Our call is to trust Him, to follow Him totally, to lay our human designs and schemes of self-made joy at the foot of the cross and learn to find our all in Him.

Is this a one-time surrender? Not for me. God's Spirit has shown me that my once-in-a-lifetime choice to surrender to Him must be followed with moment-by-moment surrender in my daily choices. I am not single, but I have my own surrenders to make. Although surrendering is often a simple thing, it is never an easy thing. "I surrender all" must be my prayer again and again. It must be yours as well.

Pleasures and Protection

As women, we have deep, feminine longings. God made us to desire the pursuit and interplay of a godly romance, to enjoy the stability and pleasure of sex as an intimate expression of monogamous love, and to embrace the opportunity to build a home and family. Will you trust God with your desires? Will you allow Him to gift you with His good plans for you? Will you accept that He has good plans for you?

Sexual purity can be particularly difficult for the fearlessly feminine single. We live in a culture that glorifies pleasure. We're told that if it feels good, it couldn't be wrong. Our desires are given more weight than our ideals of chastity. We are told that we will miss out if we don't experience the pleasures of sex. Well, that is true only when we view sex as the highest pleasure a human can know. We're programmed to think of sex in that way. But it isn't. There is something—Someone—who is more pleasurable, more desirable, more satisfying than the most perfect of human unions. God Himself. The psalmist said, "You have made known to me the path of life; you will fill me with joy in your presence, with eternal pleasures at your right hand" (Psalm 16:11).

When we lose our vision of who God is, when we seek our own joys in our own self-centered ways, sex becomes like a god to us. To live a life of purity is hard. It takes discipline. But impurity is infinitely harder on us. God's love asks these difficult things of us in order to bless and protect us.

God's love does not spare us strenuous labors. It spares us

the sorrows of sin. God's love is not less loving when it calls us to suffer. It is more loving, shielding us from greater suffering. His love did not protect His own Son, and He will not protect us from anything that will make us more like His Son.

Fearlessly feminine women do not redefine God's love according to human terms. They accept God's love on His own terms because they trust His good intentions toward them.

The longing you feel within you is good. But there is something even better—God Himself. He is worth the sacrifice of obedience and self-control. Don't lay your honor and the well-being of those you love—and even more importantly, your obedience to God—on the idolatrous altar of your personal passions. Your needs are real, but they are not ultimate reality—God is. Ask God for a heart like that of the psalmist, who said, "Whom have I in heaven but you? And earth has nothing I desire besides you" (Psalm 73:25). The woman of faith accepts God's love and believes in His goodness.

Listen to one woman's personal testimony about being single:

> Through no fault or choice of my own, I am unable to express my sexuality in the beauty and intimacy of Christian marriage, as God intended when He created me a sexual being in His own image. To seek to do this outside of marriage is, by the clear teaching of Scripture, to sin against God and against my own nature. As a committed Christian, then, I have no alternative but to live a life of voluntary celibacy. I must be chaste not only in body, but in mind and spirit as well. Since I am now in my 60's [sic] I think that my experience of what this means is valid. I want to go on record as having proved that for those who are committed to

do God's will, His commands are His enablings....

My whole being cries out continually for something I may not have. My whole life must be lived in the context of this never-ceasing tension. My professional life, my social life, my personal life, my Christian life—all are subject to its constant and powerful pull. As a Christian I have no choice but to obey God, cost what it may. I must trust Him to make it possible for me to honor Him in my singleness.

That this is possible, a mighty cloud of witnesses will join me to attest. Multitudes of single Christians in every age and circumstance have proved God's sufficiency in this matter. He has promised to meet our needs and He honors His word. If we seek fulfillment in Him, we shall find it. It may not be easy, but whoever said that Christian life was easy? The badge of Christ's discipleship was a cross.

Why must I live my life alone? I do not know. But Jesus Christ is Lord of my life. I believe in the sovereignty of God, and I accept my singleness from His hand. He could have ordered my life otherwise, but He has chosen not to do so. As His child, I must trust His love and wisdom.[4]

Will you trust His love and wisdom for your own situation? He will give you the grace to be chaste—fearlessly so.

Don't Lose Today

A fearlessly feminine woman is a real woman to all those around her, regardless of her marital status. She is gentle and warm and receptive, spreading grace to those whose lives she touches. She affirms others with tenderness and sensitivity. She is vulnerable and courageous at the same time. And she is a nurturer. Every woman, whether single or married, can be maternal as she offers love and comfort to the young and vulnerable with whom God connects her.

Each one of us, whether single or married, whatever our circumstances must devote our life to the glory of God. Come to God over and over again. Trust His kind intentions toward you. Whether or not you meet Mr. Wonderful tomorrow, believe in God's wonderful goodness to you. Don't lose today by living in your fantasies for tomorrow. Accept His calling for your life today.

The call to be fearlessly feminine knows no marital boundaries. Fearless femininity is equally relevant for all women at all stages of our lives. Lay your hopes and fears and longings and loneliness and impatience at the feet of the One who knows what it means to live a single life. Trust the promises of Christ so fully that joy and courage and peace overflow within your feminine soul. Then you can say with the hymn writer:

Take my love—my God, I pour
At Thy feet its treasure store.
FRANCES RIDLEY HAVERGAL, 1836–1879

Study Questions

1. If you are single and studying this in a group, share with the others how God has helped you in some of the tough times of being single.

2. Invest some time reading books either about or by these single Christians: Mary Slessor, Amy Carmichael, Luci Swindoll, Margaret Clarkson, Lottie Moon, Gladys Aylward.

3. At what point in your life is it hardest for you to be content? What confinement are you tempted to run from? (Genesis 16).

4. How can you live out your single femininity more fearlessly before those around you?

Perhaps a better woman after all, with chubby children hanging on my neck to keep me low and wise.

ELIZABETH BARRETT BROWNING

Indulgence or Cruelty?

SUSANNA WESLEY

(1669–1742)

Susanna Wesley, best known as mother of John and Charles Wesley, was eight months pregnant with her nineteenth child in 1709 when the church rectory in Epworth, England, caught fire for a second time. She had already lost nine of her children to various childhood tragedies and diseases. She nearly lost John, age six, in this fire. Who was this woman who gave us two sons who changed the face of the Christian church in the eighteenth century?

She married Samuel Wesley in 1688, and they spent most of their married life together as parson and wife in a tiny village in Lincolnshire, England. During Samuel's frequent absences, Susanna saw to the needs of the parish, farmed the church acreage, and ran her household. She made herself responsible for the education of her family and spent six hours each day teaching her children once they reached the age of five. All three of her sons became recognized scholars, and one of her daughters could read New Testament Greek at the age of eight.

Susanna made a set of rules that all the children were required to follow with care. She refused to let a minute be wasted. All ten of her children were raised with a very real sense of right and wrong. She wrote:

> The subjecting of the will (of a child) is a thing which must be done at once, and the sooner the better; for by neglecting timely correction they will contract a stubbornness and obstinacy which are hardly ever after conquered, and never without using such severity as

would be painful to me as to the child. In the esteem of the world they pass for kind and indulgent, whom I call cruel parents: who permit their children to get habits which they know must afterwards be broken.[1]

She made a practice of retiring to her bedchamber each afternoon at five o'clock for one hour of prayer, meditation, and writing while the younger children were minded by the older ones. Her children held her in highest esteem and affection and sought her guidance in various difficulties. She prayed constantly for them and kept up a lively correspondence throughout her life.

When Samuel Wesley died in 1735, Susanna found it necessary to sell everything to pay off their debts. Her son John was hesitant to take a new ministry across the ocean in the new colony of Georgia because of her poverty. Should he not stay in England and help support his mother? "Had I twenty sons, I should rejoice that they were all so employed, though I should never see them more."[2] She was a woman who gave her life to her children, and then gave her children to the Lord.

CHAPTER SIX

Courageously Cherishing our Children

M y mother was the strongest influence in my childhood world. She introduced me to life and won my love while requiring respect. My earliest memory—I must have been almost three years old—is of being awakened from my afternoon nap by my baby sister's crying. Pati and I shared a room, and I remember my first feelings of jealousy welling up when I saw our mother bringing my little sister a bottle to comfort her. Afraid that I might be scolded, but missing the days when that crib and bottle had been all mine, I asked my mother for a bottle, too. I still remember the relief and security I felt when Mom understood my needs. She didn't worry about spoiling me—she heard my heart's longing in that childish request. She gently lifted me into the crib, brought me a bottle of my own, and then asked me to watch over my baby sister for a little while. Her maternal comfort and love filled me with a security that started shaping my soul at a very young age.

I want to talk with you about the privilege, the price, and the power of cherishing our children. While this chapter is addressed to mothers, please read it even if you are not one yet. Whether you have children of your own or relate to them as an aunt, teacher, friend, or neighbor, I want to encourage you to be fearlessly feminine in your relationships with children. How the children need us—in our neighborhoods, schools, churches, and communities. Life would be barren without the powerful influence of women mothering: nurturing, leading, teaching, valuing, correcting, cherishing those children God brings into our lives.

Deborah was an Israelite judge who helped lead the nation to victory over the Canaanites. In her song of victory, she sang, "Village life in Israel ceased, ceased until I, Deborah, arose, arose a mother in Israel" (Judges 5:7). "A mother in Israel"— what an interesting way to describe her role at that point in history. She accepted the maternal challenge to counsel, support, and encourage those around her. She knew the ways of the Lord, and she declared them with courage and clarity (Judges 4:4–16). Where are the "mothers in Israel" of today? Who will nurture the next generation? Who will embrace the privilege, pay the price, and make good use of the power of courageous mothering to bring life to the children in their sphere of influence?

The Privilege of Motherhood

Will you embrace the privilege of mothering? As Mr. Rogers, the soft-spoken host of PBS's *Mr. Rogers' Neighborhood*, sings, "Only girls can be the mommies." What a privilege to welcome into our bodies and hearts those new human lives that will forever change the way we live and love. The very essence of femininity—the gentle grace of serving others with beauty and joy—is most clearly seen when we mother. Motherhood calls for the best in us as women. We are not merely biological reproducers. As women we can set the emotional tone and nourish the heart of our homes. As mothers we shape the souls of our children and ultimately influence the world.

Think of the honor of guiding the spiritual, intellectual, and social development of young hearts and minds. Think of the thrill of teaching your child the eternal truths of God's Word. Think of the delight of seeing your child defer to the desire of another or tell the truth despite the prospect of punishment or express love with clarity and sincerity. Think of the privilege of sending one more godly, vibrant, strong, young man or woman into this sin-saddened world with the courage to live life well for Christ's sake.

Children are our investment in the future. They will bear the imprint of our mothering throughout their lives. As mothers, we teach our children all the values we believe must be passed on to the next generation: love, faithfulness, trust, obedience, respect, honesty, loyalty. Through our mothering, we allow them to taste the value of commitment and relish the peace of security. In us they experience what the world should be like. We are life's mirrors to our children, reflecting warmth and friendship. When we mother well, we teach our children to embrace the moral obligations that build solid relationships, healthy marriages, and secure families. Oh, what a sacred gift it is when a woman receives the title Mother! There is no higher calling.

A mother has the privilege of developing a sense of self in her child. Self-worth is a reflection of how God and those around us view us. Am I a burden? Unwanted? Unappreciated? Or am I loved with a love that cannot be broken? Is someone totally committed to me? Do I bring someone joy?

My own dear mother loves me unconditionally. She always

thinks the best of me. She is my biggest fan. I would not be writing this book were it not for her. Her life taught me that children are a rare treasure to be highly valued. She fearlessly embraced the privilege of motherhood.

God is calling us women to embrace the privilege of maternal care. We will not hear this from the culture of convenience surrounding us. A woman is much more likely to be praised for her work in the marketplace than for her commitment to mothering. And if mothering is not honored, women will stop doing it. Today if a baby seems to be too great a burden, either financially or physically or emotionally, a woman may kill it in what should be the safest place this side of heaven, a mother's womb. Or, once it is born, she may throw it in the trash bin so she can get on with the important things in life—like attending the prom or satisfying her pubescent boyfriend.

Where are the women who will fearlessly surrender to the privilege of motherhood? Who will say, "My child's welfare is more important than my own convenience; I will give my child a sense of God; I will protect my child from evil and death; I will set the highest possible standards of honor and morality for my child to follow as I teach him the Bible, and one day I will send him out with a light in his soul to bless this darkened world"?* What greater privilege could we have?

Your role in a child's life—whether it is your child or others around you—is invaluable. You can be the one to teach him to form intimate, emotional bonds with others. Your sensitivity, availability, devotion, affection, unhurried attention, and responsiveness are irreplaceable. You have the joy of creating

*For greater ease in reading I will use only the masculine pronoun, but, as a mother of both sons and a daughter, I urge you to think in terms of both sexes as you read.

an environment for discovery and growth and imagination. You have the privilege of training your child to resist the me-centered consumerism that engulfs our world today. To be fearlessly feminine in our mothering means to have a deep sense of purpose and conviction that to be a mother is one of God's greatest gifts. *Embrace the privilege* of mothering.

The Price of Motherhood

Second, will you *pay the price* of mothering? In *Where Have All the Mothers Gone?* Brenda Hunter cites numerous studies showing that every child needs someone to make an "irrational" commitment to him; someone who will be there when she is needed; someone who will not pack up and go home at 6:00 P.M. Additionally, this someone must love the child more than other people's children.[3] Who can do this better than a child's own mother? Yet we hear the chorus swelling around us, "The care of children and home are inferior occupations. The marketplace is more rewarding. Find your worth there."

And so we face a decision. Don't let me heap guilt on your head if you *must* work outside your home while your children are young. I have been there, and I know how hard it is. I am writing about a decision that a working mom makes who has a *choice* to cut back and stay home with her children. Are we willing to give up the pluses of the working world for diapers, doctor appointments, feeding schedules, and hurried showers? We enjoy the affirmations of working outside the home—a paycheck, pats on the back, exciting challenges, and new relationships—and yet we know that our home life suffers all the while. We begin to realize that all the tangible successes in the marketplace can never mask the potent pull of mother love.

But are we women enough to yield to this powerful force?

When Ray and I were first married, I taught a multi-age (second and third grade) class for four years in the inner city of Dallas while he attended seminary. My work was tiring, sometimes frightening, but very rewarding. Yet I knew it was temporary, because Ray and I both believed that once God granted us children, I should pour all my energies into our home life.

After Ray's graduation we moved to Palo Alto, California, where he served on the pastoral staff of a large church. Soon Eric was born and then Krista and then Dane, all in less than three years. Gavin didn't arrive until four years later. I found myself surprised at the exhausting and inescapable demands of mothering. What a high cost these babies were exacting from me! Somehow the realities of raising young children had never entered my motherhood fantasies.

I thought that teaching twenty-eight energetic and needy children how to read had to be the hardest job on earth. I was wrong—mothering was. Now I had to give up my right to sleep when I needed it, to a meal without interruptions, to relaxation when I wanted it, and most importantly, my right to withdraw when I felt overwhelmed.

Motherhood is costly. And it is only natural to try to resist the pain and still reap the benefits. But it is this very difficulty, surmounted and conquered, that brings the richest rewards. Anything of worth is costly: devotion to Christ, a strong marriage, financial responsibility, a life of integrity, and of course, fearlessly feminine mothering.

To be fearlessly feminine means mothering well. It means being willing to put someone else's needs ahead of your own. The fearlessly feminine woman stops running from her children. She develops a deep sense of the value of her hourly sacrifices as a mother. There is no "National Mothers' Union" she can petition for higher pay or better work conditions. Yet as she surrenders to the call of motherhood, she fleshes out her answer to the question, "What is truly important in my life; what is of eternal significance?"

The price of motherhood is high. A mother gives her heart, her time, her energy—both emotional and physical—when she mothers well. But it is in this wholehearted giving that she becomes her best as a woman. Brenda Hunter, in another excellent book, *The Power of Mother Love,* calls this the "power of surrender." She says:

> Surrendering to mother love, then, means giving your child your love, your time, and your attention when he needs it. It means choosing to live your life in such a way that you are physically present and emotionally available for large chunks of "quantity" time, even when it's inconvenient. It means making difficult choices—professional, financial, and personal choices—so that you can be *with* your child in body, heart, mind, and soul. It may mean postponing your dreams. It will definitely mean making sacrifices[4]

Are you willing to pay the price? Kids cost, but they're worth it.

My friend Suzanne proves how much our children deserve our best. Suzanne is a creative, energetic, compassionate young woman who developed a sterling reputation as a student teacher and teacher's aide in a Chicago district where positions are highly coveted. She became a personal friend when she discipled our daughter, Krista, during Krista's high school years.

When Suzanne and her husband, Scott, had their first baby, they made the hard decision to have Suzanne leave the market-place to mother full-time. What is the result? Five-year-old Tyler is an obedient, confident, bright boy—a joy to be around. And three-year-old Krista (our daughter's namesake), is a secure, impishly tenacious, totally irresistible little girl. Both Tyler and Krista have strong wills and have required hard work, patience, and untold sacrifices on the part of their parents. But if you could spend an afternoon with these little ones, as my family loves to do, you would see the imprint of their mother on them, and you would delight in it. Has it been easy? Definitely not. Suzanne has felt depleted, isolated, and financially strapped at times. But to her the price has been worth it. She could never replace those years with her babies, nor would she want to. How much value would any other success hold if she failed as a mother?

Someone is going to be influencing your child during those formative preschool years. *Someone* is going to be inculcating values and imprinting standards on that impressionable young soul. Let it be *you*. Make the effort to create an atmosphere where faith and obedience can be nurtured, where love and security are readily accessible. This takes time—continual exposure and intervention. It isn't easy. But God's purpose for us as His daughters is not freedom from the difficulties in life. His goal is to make us like Christ and, through us, to mark our children with His beauty. He intends to conform us to the image of His Son (Romans 8:29). What is that image? Philippians 2 tells us that Christ was obedient to God's call, humbling Himself, considering others before Himself, *all the way to the cross*. Christ Himself said, "And whoever wants to become great among you must be your servant, and whoever wants to be first must be slave of all. For even the Son of Man did not come to be served, but to serve, and to give his life as a ransom for many" (Mark 10:43–44).

More than anywhere else, motherhood is where a woman learns to serve. It reminds me of the toddler who, while looking at his parents' wedding pictures, asked his daddy, "So, is that the day Mommie came to work for us?" We feel like that at times, don't we? Like slaves. I wonder if we resist our duties as moms, paying someone else to do it, because it is such hard work. We resent being the one "on call," who rarely gets a break. We need to accept our role as a mom—including that of slave laborer! When we're struggling with the demands and responsibilities of motherhood, our deepest problem is not necessarily an insensitive husband, cranky kids, or a tight budget. Our deepest problem is our own resistance to total selflessness. It costs to serve. It's tiring and dirty and inglorious.

Are you struggling with your role as a mother-servant in your home? Are you resenting your kids? Are you fearful that life might slip through your fingers? Recognize your feelings for what they are: self-centered and unfaithful toward the God who called you to mother. These emotions are the opposite of what is good and true and pure and kind. You may fear you'll miss out on certain things if you decide to pay the price of real motherhood. Well, of course, you *will* miss out on *some* things. An Indian proverb says it well: "Children bind the mother's feet." You won't be as free as women who reject their children. You will need to tell yourself the same things you tell your child when he is struggling with jealousy and discontentment: Jealousy never satisfies an angry heart. It only feeds discontent. God places a high value on hard work (1 Thessalonians 4:11–12). He wants us to learn contentment whatever the circumstances

(Philippians 4:11). And He promises to watch over us (Hebrews 13:5–6).

But what a trade-off. It is the hardest work you'll ever do for the greatest earthly treasures possible. Sleepless nights, peanut butter on the new sofa, and constant commotion are well worth all the joys poured back into a mother's heart. Now that our children are older, we are enjoying some of those trade-offs.

Ray taught the children at an early age to verbalize their love for me. For various family celebrations he and the kids have made cards or written me letters. Through the years I have kept a file of their precious expressions of love. When I grow weary, I look into my "Trade-Off File" to remind myself that no cost is too great to mother these four priceless gifts from God. Here's a peek into that file:

HAPPY BIRTHDAY to a *real* thin Mom, (not to mention kind-hearted, sweet, loving, beautiful, hardworking...) I could go on forever! I love you. Thanks so much for being my mom. I feel like I haven't seen you much lately, so maybe we could do something this weekend, even if it's just around the house.

With love,
Gavin (age 12)

P.S. I know you're on a diet, but it's your birthday, so—PARTY!

Or this Mother's Day poem from Dane when he was 13:

How I love thee, you really are the best,
my sweet, fair Mother Ortlund.
If I were you, and had to live with me,

I think I'd move to Portland...
But I'm not you, I'm me, you're you,
of that I'm quite relieved,
And I'll tell you the reason for that statement,
I can't quite mother like thee!!!

You do so much for me, Mom. Clean the house, give me money for lunch and haircuts...put up with me!!! I really appreciate these things even if sometimes I don't express that appreciation as clearly as I should. I don't know how I could become an adult without you being there for me. I couldn't ask for a better mom. I love you very much. Thanks for *always* being there for me and *never* letting me down. I love you.

Your son,
Dane

When our daughter, Krista, went away to college, she wrote me this:

One of the most valuable things I am learning about myself is how much I truly love you and Dad. I desperately miss you. Mom, you have given your whole life over to the Lord and the tasks He wants you to complete. One of those is your family, and you have joyfully and willingly sacrificed for each one of us. Thank you for your selfless, servant-like attitude. Thank you for your patient guidance. Mom, you are the most influential person in my life. Besides the Lord, I look to no one else for love, guidance, encouragement, and wisdom. I consider you my best friend. You are the most precious gift from God. I praise Him daily for you in my life. How can I encourage you and be the friend and daughter you need? I love you more than words can say.

Love always,
Krista

And from our oldest son, Eric:

I am so indebted to you.... You selflessly have given all of the time and energy you possess to make the Ortlund children's childhood a happy and memorable one. You have so inspired me to a cheerful, positive, calm attitude toward each day as I face it. You really honor God in your conduct toward us as a family. Your example is one that I am eager and enthusiastic to make an attempt to follow.

I love you very dearly,
Eric

Was I a perfect mother? No way! Did I get tired and cranky and lose heart at times? Yes, definitely! Did I deserve all these kind words? Absolutely not! But somehow our children saw through my mistakes and failures to my desire to be there for them. They valued my sacrifices despite my imperfections.

Listen to one young mother's expression of her willingness to pay the price of mothering:

I celebrated my little Una's third birthday by presenting her with a new brother. Both the children welcomed him with delight that was of itself compensation enough for all it cost me to get up such a celebration. Martha takes a most prosaic view of this proceeding, in which she detects *malice aforethought* on my part. She says I shall now have one mouth the more to fill, and two feet the more to shoe; more disturbed nights, more laborious days, and less leisure for visiting, reading, music, and drawing. Well! This is one side of the story, to be sure, but I look at the other. Here is a sweet, fragrant mouth to kiss; here are two more feet to make music with their pattering about my nursery. Here is a soul to train for God, and the body in which it dwells is worthy all it will cost, since it is the abode of a kingly tenant. I may see less of my friends, but I have gained one dearer than them all, to whom, while I minister in Christ's name, I make a willing sacrifice of what little leisure for my own recreation my other darlings had left me. Yes, my precious baby, you are welcome to your mother's heart, welcome to her time, her strength, her health, her most tender cares, to her lifelong prayers! Oh, how rich I am, how truly, how wondrously blest![5]

The price you will pay for mothering will fade into insignificance as your children grow. So take heart. Your own agenda can wait. Invest yourself in something greater. Pay the price to gain something richer. "Let us not become weary in doing good, for at the proper time we will reap a harvest if we do not give up" (Galatians 6:9).

The Power of Motherhood

Third, make full use of the power of motherhood. God has given you an authoritative place in the hearts of your children. You are the shaper of their souls. You are cultivating and forming the next generation. You are preparing them for future relationships as you teach them about love and trust. You must provide for them a defense of truth. You are called to be their chief mediator for goodness. They must grow up learning that virtue, obedience, and kindness are not matters of preference—they are eternal mandates from their heavenly Father. Offer to them your constant love, heartfelt sympathy, and faithful protection. Be the one to teach them how to respect their daddy and love their siblings, how to choose good nutrition and wholesome entertainment, how to value cleanliness and courtesy, and which fights are worthy of their efforts, their reputations, their very blood.

You are the most important influence in your child's life. You can build in him principles for the years ahead. You can give him resources for success in those difficult years of decision-making when his responsibilities will expand

- from cleaning his room, to caring for his own home;
- from being kind to a friend, to being understanding and sympathetic with his mate;
- from showing respect to an adult guest in your home, to cheerfully working under his supervisor at work.

For this powerful force of love between you and your child to have its fullest effect, you need to study him. This takes time—constant exposure day after day. Play with him, read to him, eat with him, nap with him, walk with him, get down on his level, and explore life through his eyes. I liked to look at each of my babies as a tiny castle. My job was to win their trust so that they would lower their emotional drawbridges, giving me access into the deepest part of their souls.

There is no great mystery to this bonding. It takes time and maternal warmth and more time and affection and more time and shared laughter and more time and shared tears and more time. Don't resist your baby's intrusions into your life. Welcome them as gateways into his heart. You are helping him develop an inner sense of his own worthiness and a capacity for intimacy that will blossom in other relationships all his life.

So remain approachable. Sympathize with your child. Be as gracious and merciful as you would want your husband or friend to be toward you, so that your child learns that you are a safe place in times of need. I believe that it is the power of a mother's love that develops the truest and best side of a child's nature. As mothers, we accept a large portion of the responsibility of sowing the seeds for tomorrow's world. What harvest will we reap?

There is so much we must do to prepare our children for the emotional, spiritual, theological, and historic battles they will face. Individualism, materialism, lack of self-restraint, and a drive to pursue pleasure at any price are the forces demanding our children's time and loyalty. As a public school teacher, I saw these forces at work even in seven- and eight-year-olds.

Children have an underdeveloped capacity for compassion. They are often rude and crude. Good manners and courtesy are foreign to them. Many have a contempt for material things, possessing much, but caring about little. Children are naturally impatient, lacking the stamina to see things through. This can develop into a pattern of incompleteness and the tendency to run away when they encounter a challenge or obstacle. As a fearlessly feminine mother, you have the power to turn your child's loyalty away from these destructive forces.

Think about the world of entertainment that engulfs young people today. Life's highest attainments are perceived as experiencing fun and happiness. We are a nation of superficial pleasure seekers. Consider two of our most highly paid professions: acting and sports. They symbolize to us the "ideal life" of megamoney and celebrity. Many children have unlimited access to their world of glamor through TV, music, and videos. In this atmosphere our children are influenced to minimize pain by pursuing pleasure. Earthly pleasure has become their ideal. "If it feels good, do it."

No wonder our children are using drugs and sex to escape from their pain—we have trained them for it. We are becoming more self-indulgent and hungry for immediate gratification. We resist tasks that require sustained application and discipline.

As mothers we must rise up and stem the flow. The fearlessly feminine mother has power that no Hollywood producer has—the power to shape patient, compassionate, courageous children, ready to lead the next generation. Let's talk about how to sow the seeds for this kind of harvest.

You can take full advantage of your powerful influence as a mother by disciplining your child and training him in righteousness. The nature of each and every child is wayward and needs correction. "Folly is bound up in the heart of a child, but the rod of discipline will drive it far from him" (Proverbs 22:15).

Without a clear sense of right and wrong enforced in the home, a child becomes easily upset and falls victim to his own errant emotions. If a child never learns to submit to a firm No! in his early years, he won't cope well with disappointments later on. Without good discipline, your child will become a moral cripple, impeded and disadvantaged in how to embrace all of life. Don't be afraid to discipline your child. God isn't. Love and discipline are the two most important things you can give your child. Proverbs 13:24 says, "He who spares the rod hates his son, but he who loves him is careful to discipline him."

We discipline on two fronts—both corrective and preventive, chastening and instructing. It's somewhat like tending a garden: My azaleas need both pruning for better growth and a good dose of fertilizer at their roots to feed them way down deep for future blossoms. Children need both careful pruning and healthy food for their souls. As a mother you have the power to create in your home an environment that can provide both. It will require hard work, creativity, and a strong sense of your call as a mother. But what is the alternative? "A child left to himself disgraces his mother" (Proverbs 29:15).

Your goal as a mother is to raise children who will be responsible, godly adults who will bring a rich, life-giving texture to their homes, churches, and communities. They must be able to face the world with courage and independence and be skillful in making wise decisions regarding friends, entertainment, and money. To achieve this goal your child must have the luxury of hours under your influence. You must control his TV and Nintendo time. You must be willing to make mealtime a priority and protect your family time at any cost.

How do you train a child to be a mature, patient adult who is not always focused on his own needs, who can control his spending, and who can save sex for his marriage partner alone? It must start at a very young age, both through example and instruction. Children must learn early on to control their selfish impulses: not to hit in order to get what they want, to obey instructions, to cooperate, and to share. They need to learn to inhibit their urge to gratify their impulses. And they need to learn these things from *you*. It is your duty and privilege to train your child. God matched you up with your particular children for a reason.

Child training will not change a child's heart (only God can do that), but it will change how he expresses what is in his heart. Child training includes the directing and shaping of a child's words and actions in every sphere of his life. It is a mistake to think that your chief duty in training your children is to love them and simply *show* them what they ought to do. Your chief duty is to love them and *make* them do what they ought to do. Don't take it for granted that if your child is overly shy or embarrassingly aggressive or one-sided in any way, that he must remain that way. Each child is unique, but it is not inevitable that he should continue to exhibit disagreeable peculiarities in offensive ways. Children can be trained in almost any direction. It is the privilege and duty of the fearlessly feminine mother, by God's grace, to make her children be and do what they *should* be and do rather than what they *want* to be and do.

Principles of Mothering

Let me offer some principles that Ray and I have found helpful in training our four children:

1. *Define your priorities.* What's really important to you? What would you go to the mat for? Some of the qualities that we hold high in our home are: self-control, kindness, courtesy, integrity, honesty, hard work, gen-

erosity, respect. Don't spin your wheels on the unimportant things—save your energy for the important issues.

2. *Make your life an example for your children.* It must be just as much "Be what I am" as it is "Do what I say." Discipline is for parents first. That is why it is so hard. But disciplined mothers raise disciplined children. Hopefully we can say to our children, just as Gideon said to his men in Judges 7:17, "Watch me.... Follow my lead.... Do exactly as I do."

3. *Study your child.* Child training is limited in every case by the child's capacity. Training your child requires studying him. Know your child; look into his eyes often and deeply. Touch him; talk with him; observe him in a variety of situations. Ponder long and well such questions as:

- Where is he weakest/strongest?
- Which of his strengths is most likely to lead him astray or fail him?
- What needs immediate attention?
- What deserves praise?
- What *won't* he be doing when he's sixteen? In other words, try to distinguish between childishness and character traits, what he'll leave behind and what he'll carry with him into adulthood.

4. *Be careful not to crush your child.* A child's will ought to be strong for doing right; but if it isn't, we don't

want to train by brute force alone. We must feed his soul so that he himself is ready to choose in favor of the right. We must never crush his will through verbal or physical intimidation. Our ultimate goal is to train him to choose right for himself, from the heart, even when Mom isn't around.

5. *Teach your child to control himself.* When we say no to our preschoolers, they can say no to themselves when they're older. Hearing "no!" and surviving the frustration that automatically comes with it gives kids strength. It builds endurance and helps them control their frustrations and impulses. It helps them learn to delay gratification. Proverbs 29:11 says, "A fool gives full vent to his anger, but a wise man keeps himself under control."

6. *Require obedience.* Say yes whenever you possibly can. But when you say no, mean it. For young children especially, your instructions are not the first bid in a negotiations process. If you must discipline, make the pain of the discipline outweigh the pleasure of disobedience, or it will be meaningless to your child. For a child to change his ways, it must be more unpleasant to follow his own impulse than to obey you when he doesn't feel like it. Require quick, cheerful obedience. Obeying with a pout or an argument is not true obedience.

Children argue with us for two reasons: We let them, and they think they can win. But your home is not a democracy. God has given you the authority. Are rebel forces taking over at your house?

I remember one of my students who surprised me with his candor about whom he would obey. Tommy (not his real name) was a particularly difficult child, whose reputation for obnoxious, defiant, disruptive behavior had me nervous even before he entered my classroom. I was determined, however, not to let a little seven-year-old run my class or ruin my year.

As the weeks passed, I found myself making headway with this brilliant little tyrant. Through daily behavior charts and rewards, strong support from his mother, exhausting creative energy, and sheer feminine stubbornness, I was able to get Tommy to become a participating member of the class.

The reason for my apparent success wasn't clear to me until an incident took place in his gym class. As I came to pick up my students, his PE teacher, who happens to be six feet four inches and can be rather intimidating, motioned me aside. He let me know that Tommy had refused to take off his shoes and stand on the scale to get weighed. I had to meet this challenge! A coworker watched my class while I marched Tommy back to the scales and with a few sparks flying, demanded that he do as he was told. He did. On the way back to our room I asked him, "Tommy, why did you have to take me from my other students? Why wouldn't you do this for your PE teacher?"

His quick reply was, "I didn't think he would make me, but I knew YOU would."

Elisabeth Elliot, in a letter to her daughter, writes of the importance of obedience.

From the day you were born, almost, I tried to teach you that the word I spoke was the word I meant. It was to be taken seriously, to be lived by, in your child-life. How shall we learn to believe and obey God if we have not been taught from earliest childhood to believe and obey the ones He puts over us? A child has to know first of all and beyond any shadow of doubt that the word spoken will be the word carried out.[6]

Require obedience. Carry out your word. This will mean hope and life for your child. "Discipline your son, for in that there is hope; do not be a willing party to his death" (Proverbs 19:18).

7. *Teach respect for other people and for property.* Moms are the key to this. Respect starts in the home. Never let your child sass you or put you down. When a child respects his mother, he learns to listen to those in authority over him. He learns to bend and flex without undue agitation. He experiences an order and pattern to life that provides security and stability. If a child respects his mother, he usually has an easier time respecting his teachers, his neighbors, and others over him. All of society benefits.

A child must also learn to respect property. Some kids seem bent on destruction. We do them and their community a favor when we restrain them. Some people believe that when a child destroys a toy, it is enough punishment for him to have to live with the consequences; i.e., he won't have his toy anymore. I think it is a rare child who destroys something he really likes. Destructiveness is selfishness. The child is saying by his actions, "I just want to do what I want to do." Respect means that boundaries are set for expressions of anger and frustration.

By learning respect at a young age, children see that people and things should not be targets for their wrath. There must be no childish uncontrolled contempt for people and things in the home of the fearlessly feminine mother who truly cherishes her child.

8. *Teach hard work.* Every child learns his work ethic at home, most probably from his mother. From a very early age, a child should be a helping member of the family unit. This requires patient, creative, structured teaching from his mother. First, you do it for him. Then, you do it together. Finally, he does it himself. Don't skip or shorten the "together" step. He will learn how to work as he watches you and works with you. Refuse to allow a whining or complaining spirit to creep into these moments. Correct it with your godly, cheerful example and clear instruction from God's Word about our responsibilities as Christians.

9. *Give many rewards.* Punishment teaches what not to do. You want to teach your child that good and pleasure go together, just as surely as sin and pain. That's how we learn to fear and hate sin. Reward kindness, good deeds, and cheerful obedience.

Enhance your relationship with your child by

making lots of deposits in his "love bank." Then when you need to make a withdrawal through discipline, your relationship won't go bankrupt.

10. *Forget guilt trips.* We all make mistakes, children and parents alike. Children would rather live with a parent who makes an occasional mistake than with one who never cares enough to discipline them at all. John White speaks to our guilt as parents in his helpful book *Parents in Pain:*

> Make it the aim of your life then to adopt God's standard and leave the results of doing so with him. Bring him your loaves and fishes telling him it is all that you have, but look at what he demands you do with the loaves and fishes. It is not your responsibility to make sure five thousand stomachs are filled. It is your responsibility to obey instructions. Beside the Sea of Galilee, it meant to go on breaking and passing bread as long as the supply lasted. As a parent of growing children, it means that you will go on striving to be to your children all that God is to you. It is God's part to look after the miracles.[7]

These are dangerous days for our children. Students are being murdered by their classmates; they are being taught that life is only worthy when it is healthy, wealthy, and wanted and that their highest goal should be to minimize their pain by pursuing pleasures regardless of the consequences to others. Our children need their mothers. We must recommit ourselves to nurture and train the next generation. We must embrace the privilege, pay the price, and wield the power of motherhood. The mother love you feel begging to express itself is springing from the very core of your femininity. Cultivate it; demonstrate it. Let us pour our time and energy into our children. Let us not neglect what God has called us to do or ignore what He has called us to be as women. Let us fearlessly engage ourselves in the difficult and challenging profession of motherhood.

Let me conclude with a prophetic word from a fearless woman, who just happens to be the mother of my husband. (Thanks for the *great* job you did, Mom!)

> We must remember our original calling to be women.
> Whatever the sacrifice, we must get back to the basics,
> to what God has called us to be and do as women—
> which only we, and nobody else, can be and do.[8]

Cherish your children. Welcome the privilege of motherhood. Submit to the sacrifices of mothering. Exercise your power as a mother. Apply the principles of mothering. Doing so may be the clearest example of fearless femininity in our world today.

Study Questions

1. How does the assurance of Proverbs 29:17 encourage you as you are raising your children right now?

2. Make a list of those things you can do for your child that no one else can do. These are your privileges as a mother.

3. Where is it hardest for you to pay the price of motherhood? What struggles are you facing?

4. Describe each of your children.

5. What spiritual, emotional, and cultural battles is your family facing these days? What does God's Word have to say to you in your struggles?

6. Write down at least one new direction you want to take as a mother.

A hundred men may make an encampment,
but it takes a woman to make a home.

CHINESE PROVERB

A Shelter for Seekers
EDITH SCHAEFFER
(1914–)

Edith Schaeffer, noted author of sixteen books and popular speaker all over the world, was born in China to missionary parents in 1914. One of her early memories, made even more vivid because she was the third daughter in her family, was that of walking past a pagoda along the Wenchow city wall and hearing whimpers. This was the place where unwanted newborn baby girls were thrown away. When in her distress she asked her Amah "Why?" the answer came, "These people don't know about God, or about Jesus His Son. That is why your parents came to China."[1]

Edith Schaeffer has spent her life answering people's questions about God and the whys of life. In 1948 she and her husband, Dr. Francis Schaeffer, were sent to Europe as missionaries, and seven years later they settled in Switzerland where they founded *L'Abri* ("The Shelter") *Fellowship*. Throughout their thirty years of ministry at *L'Abri*, at first hundreds and then thousands of young people arrived each year, seeking answers and needing shelter. Whether washing and ironing, nursing the sick, caring for her own four children, or baking for a crowd, Edith was always willing to take the time to give answers about the God who exists. "This is what we felt we were being led to do: to ask God that our work, and our lives be a demonstration that He does exist."[2]

Her lifelong love of literature, art, and the humanities and her creativity in building a real home for seekers made her especially well equipped to answer the questions of the rebellious students who came to her and her husband for answers.

While presiding over the hospitality side of their ministry, she also welcomed the important one-on-one encounters with searching young people. "To the thousands of young people who looked to her for help, she was on call twenty-four hours a day. To anyone in need of spiritual answers or emotional and intellectual help, Edith Schaeffer's door was never shut."[3]

Edith settled in Rochester, Minnesota, after Francis's death from cancer in 1984. Believing that Christianity is truth and not just a religious experience, she has continued to minister to her children, her spiritual children, and her readers through her patient, gentle answers to their questions.

CHAPTER SEVEN

Domestic Devotion

I n recent decades the feminist perspective has influenced much of our public discourse on marriage and family. Consequently, a view of women has developed that stereo-types the homemaker's role as undesirable. We have been bombarded with images that draw from us a certain contempt for the "housewife" and her lack of selfhood. The homemaker is sometimes portrayed as parasitical and without social or individual worth. She is perceived as needing little intelligence since her duties are routine and narrow in scope and inherently uninteresting, undemanding, and unnecessary.[4]

This is not a chapter on whether a woman should ever work outside her home, because the Bible gives us no hard and fast rules on this subject. This is a chapter calling women to a deeper understanding of the vital and eternal significance of our homes. It is an invitation to women to face without fear the pervading ethos that extols the ideal of women seeking fulfillment in full-time careers outside their homes and accepts without question the reality that the children of these mothers will receive part-time mothering. It is a plea that we as Christian women would learn to value our maternal and domestic roles above our careers.

A Worthy Occupation

I have been married for twenty-eight years and have worked full-time outside our home for twelve of those years. For the first four years of our marriage I taught public school in the inner city of Dallas. When our babies started coming, I left teaching to become a stay-at-home mom and was able to be with our four children full-time for the next fifteen years. But then it became necessary for me to go back to work. This was a very difficult decision for Ray and me.

We had moved to Illinois when Ray was called to a teaching ministry at a seminary. We thought we could make it financially in this expensive Chicago suburb if we were frugal. So we downsized from our house in Oregon. Our three boys shared a bedroom, and we limited the six of us to one car to keep costs down. I substituted in area schools and tutored and taught piano lessons as well. Ray supplemented our income with speaking and writing.

But after a few months, it became obvious that the basic needs of our growing family were exceeding our income. What should we do? Our children were settling in nicely to their new schools, and we hated to disrupt the three older ones (ages twelve, thirteen, and fourteen), who had already changed educational systems three times in their young lives. For this and other reasons, neither Ray nor I felt it would be a good decision to move to a cheaper area where we could live on his salary alone. But should I go to work full-time during these irreplaceable years? Through much prayer, advice, and even some tears, I sought employment and was offered a position in the elementary school system of our town. I taught second grade for eight years—years of fatigue and frustrations, but also years of joy and growth for us as a family.

I say this not as an example of what anyone else should do or not do. Each family is unique and is called by God to fulfill His individual plan for them. Rather, I say it to let you know I have been on both sides—a stay-at-home mom engaged in cottage industries and a go-to-work mom with four active, needy kids. And I have suffered what many of you working mothers have agonized over—the secret, silent bleeding of a working mother's heart, with all the accompanying guilt and exhaustion and divided loyalties.

But the real issue isn't what I have experienced, though it may help build a bridge to you as a reader. The question isn't even whether or not a woman should work outside her home. The question goes deeper than that. Anne Ortland shows that the real issue is this: What does the Bible say about women working?

The Bible certainly doesn't say women can't work. Lydia was a dealer in expensive purple fabric (Acts 16:14). Aquila and Priscilla were a married couple in business together (Acts 18:3). Dorcas was a dressmaker—although maybe not for salary (Acts 9:36, 39). The woman of Proverbs 31 bought and sold property and clothing and who knows what else (vv. 13–27). But the Bible has everything to say about seeking first God's kingdom. It has strong words about not letting concern for food and clothes get in the way of following His principles.[5]

Here is the issue: How can I best live my life to seek first God's kingdom? What really is worth pouring my life into? What do I most desire to see when I look back upon the years of my life here on earth? What pattern am I displaying to those in my home and church and community? What legacy am I leaving for those God has called me to nurture?

Only God can define what is truly significant as we live this earthly life. Affirmation and significance are what we're looking for, but are we seeking them in the wrong places? Are we lured into thinking that a career will meet our needs? We're tempted to pursue fulfillment and happiness in self-development. We look inward and define ourselves by what we do. And if what we do takes us outside our homes, we are given more prestige, which in turn makes us feel that the care of our homes and children are inferior occupations. The status of the full-time homemaker has been eroded. And when the home is undervalued, some women choose wage earning over childrearing and homemaking.

In *The Second Shift: Working Parents and the Revolution at Home,* Arlie Hochshild explores the difficulties of women working full-time outside their homes (whether of necessity or by choice). She blames our escalating divorce rate on discord over the "second shift" in two-income families. Women, she says, are just as tired as men when they get home from work; therefore, men and women should share equally in all household management and duties. Anger, frustration, and resentment grow over an unequal division of duties. Hochshild says that when men resist helping at home, they devalue it, and divorce is the result.[6]

Equality has risen to a sacred status in our generation. But in demanding equality, are we losing all that truly matters—our marriages, our families, our relationships, and ultimately our own happiness? Who says life is ever equal or fair? It wasn't for Jesus, and He is our pattern (Philippians 2:5–8). Proverbs 31 does not praise its heroine for her ability to get her husband to share equally in the management of their home. On the contrary, it shows a woman using her skills and creativity throughout the day and night to build a shelter for those she loves and to free her husband to fulfill God's call on his life. Our families and our homelife must never be on the periphery of our chief efforts and creative energies. It pleases God when we devote ourselves to our homes.

Think of Paul's clear and compelling advice to older women: "Train the younger women to love their husbands and children...to be busy at home" (Titus 2:3–5). The Bible clearly affirms the importance of domestic devotion. To whom and what are you devoted? Who receives the most productive hours of your day? What people are the beneficiaries of your fullest and freshest energies? It is an illusion that a woman can achieve career success without sacrificing to some degree the daily personal care of her home and her young children. When I was working outside our home, I found that both my career and our home suffered to some extent. I was torn because I couldn't give 100 percent to both callings, much as I wanted to. I found it impossible to maintain an expanding career and be the full-time mother and homemaker I desired to be.

Why do women consider fulfilling the market demands of a stranger to be of greater worth than meeting the needs of their own families? At what cost will we weaken the tie that binds a mother to her child? F. Carolyn Graglia in her critique of contemporary feminism, *Domestic Tranquility*, calls this weakening the "defeminization" of a woman.

A mother must steel herself if she is to leave her baby in a crib in a day care center or at home with a caretaker. She must suppress her longing to respond to her baby's cries and to satisfy that yearning for contact with her baby's body that her own body has been groomed to anticipate and desire. She knows, moreover, that her baby's cries will be answered by one with no special feeling of love for the child, but at most only a feeling of obligation to do as well as possible the job for which one is paid. To leave her baby requires a kind of defeminization of the woman, a constriction of the longings to be with and care for her child that is integral to woman's humanity. It requires her to develop an attitude of remoteness and withdrawal from her baby.[7]

I know that some mothers are in situations that force them to work. I have been there myself. Economic necessities, divorce, or single parenting often constrain mothers to provide financially for their children. But many women with young children choose to work for other reasons: to fulfill a dream, to escape what they consider to be sure boredom, to ensure that their career plans won't derail, to increase their standard of living. But at what cost?

The Gift of Attention

Let's be fearlessly feminine in how we approach our home duties. Let's stop the whirlwind we live in and give the gift of attention to those we love most. Let's share irreplaceable moments of peace and joy as we serve our families and mediate life to them. The formation and maintenance of a stable, godly family honors God. It can be our greatest contribution to society at large and a deep source of personal satisfaction.

Each night as Ray and I pray before going to sleep, we find ourselves grateful for many things, not the least of which are the ministry opportunities with which the Lord has blessed us. But more than anything else, we are grateful for our dear children and the direction their lives are taking. By God's grace, and despite my having had to work outside our home during part of their childhood, God has set our children on a firm foundation. We are so grateful for their solid lives. At ages twenty-three, twenty-two, twenty-one, and sixteen they are walking in paths of integrity and service. They love the Lord, and they love each other. It has been worth everything to see them settling strongly into Christ, eager to reach out, and ready to fulfill God's call to them.

My friend Diana has her doctorate in physiology. Her husband, Jim, is an orthopedic surgeon in the army. For ten years, Diana was on the faculty of a medical school on the East Coast. She was the only nonmilitary, female, full-time faculty member with a Ph.D. in the department. This intelligent, industrious woman was promoted to full professor by her midthirties, and there was even a research award established in her name.

When I first met Diana I knew nothing of this. We became friends through our car pool prayer group. When I asked Diana why she gave up her career to be a full-time homemaker and mother to her three children, she said:

> I had accomplished a lot, Jani, but nothing compares to what my family means to me. When Jim took a fellowship, we had to give up certain things, including my teaching and research. But I have no regrets looking

back. Being a mother is my first calling—to love, protect, be there with my children. Our home has more of my imprint on it now. The gratification of the marketplace can't compare to sharing life with my children. They are my legacy. Yes, there are days when I feel overwhelmed, lonely, unappreciated, and unrecognized. It takes a special woman who can be content within the four walls of her house. But I know that no one can do for my kids what I am doing.

Diana is living out one of the beautiful realities of fearless femininity: Marriage and childbearing are the ultimate surrender of the feminine soul. We must never live life doing only what is right for ourselves. We must base our decisions on what is best for those we love, surrendering to their needs.

Building a Shelter

How can we best yield to our God-ordained calling? First, let's make certain we absorb more from our Bible than we do from our culture. "Do not conform any longer to the pattern of this world" (Romans 12:2). "Woe to those who call evil good and good evil" (Isaiah 5:20). "I know, my God, that you test the heart and are pleased with integrity" (1 Chronicles 29:17).

God, our wise and loving Father, created marriage and families for our blessing. He began it when He said, "It is not good for the man to be alone" (Genesis 2:18). How precious is the human family! It is the wellspring of all our deepest feelings. When Jesus wanted to calm His disciples' fears, He spoke of preparing a place for them in His Father's house (John 14:1–6). He knew that our deepest longings revolve around a place to belong, to find rest and refreshment and unconditional welcome.

I believe that a godly home is a foretaste of heaven. Our homes, imperfect as they are, must be a haven from the chaos outside. They should be a reflection of our eternal home, where troubled souls find peace, weary hearts find rest, hungry bodies find refreshment, lonely pilgrims find communion, and wounded spirits find compassion—what Robert G. Ingersoll called "a palace for the soul."

The fearlessly feminine woman makes her home her chief career. She devotes her skills and creativity primarily to managing her household. She makes a lifelong commitment to build an earthly shelter for those she loves most. She abandons her personal rights in order to invest herself in others. She understands what life is really all about, especially family life. She knows how to balance the ledger of her life in favor of those she loves.

Let us confidently accept the loving purpose of God in our lives as women. When God created me, He designed me with a unique suitability to my divinely appointed task. The most significant thing I can do with my life now is to live out before my husband and children all that God would have me be and do as His daughter. Oh, how we need a new generation of women who will refuse to sacrifice their husbands and children for the sake of their own autonomy. Ezekiel could have been speaking to our day when he said,

> You took your sons and daughters whom you bore to me and sacrificed them...to the idols.... You slaughtered my children.... Everyone...will quote this proverb about you: "Like mother, like daughter." You

are a true daughter of your mother, who despised her husband and her children. (Ezekiel 16:20–21; 44–45)

What are we teaching our daughters? What legacy are we leaving them?

To establish a godly, secure haven for our families requires persistent effort and a commitment of time. Strong families don't just happen—they take deliberate, conscious planning. "The wise woman builds her house, but with her own hands the foolish one tears hers down" (Proverbs 14:1). "The house of the righteous stands firm" (Proverbs 12:7).

If we are wise, we'll create an atmosphere where family hurts can be healed. We'll construct a shelter where weary loved ones can find rest and aged family members will be honored. We'll fashion a headquarters for the transfer of truth from one generation to the next, where honest questions can be acknowledged and the young prepared for the years ahead. We'll develop a place where the go-getters can be generously recharged, the unwise can receive godly counsel, and the successful can be liberally praised. We'll build a harbor for happiness, where all who enter will find the love and comfort necessary to thrive this side of heaven. Is your home rooted and settled in the wisdom and righteousness of God? Or do you find it shaking and wavering under the pressures of outside forces and your own diminished view of how important a stable home truly is?

When Proverbs tells us that the wise woman builds her house, it obviously doesn't mean that we must get hammer and nails and actually construct it. (Though I do have friends who have been tempted to help the construction workers move at a more timely pace!) A godly home is built with relationships.

Homemaking is about people, and the key relationship in

your home, if you're married, is your husband. God has created us as wives to be our husbands' *helpers* (Genesis 2:18). As we saw in chapter 4, a helper gives aid and assists in time of need. Happy the home where the wife understands that God created her to *complete* her husband, not *compete* with him! To be a helper is not demeaning. The fearlessly feminine wife delights to serve her husband, just as the church delights to serve Christ (Ephesians 5:23). She is absolutely dependable, bringing him only good all the days of her life (Proverbs 31:12).

But what about those women who are not married? Perhaps you're single with children. Or maybe you live alone, either hoping to fill a home with a family someday or remembering the days when your home was humming with a husband and children. Domestic devotion is for all women in all situations and in all of life's stages. Neighbors and friends, unexpected strangers and anticipated guests will all benefit from your womanly care. The human soul craves love and fellowship. You can provide shelter for the hurting and hungry. To whom will you open your door?

Human beings need a refuge from birth to death—protection from the emotional, intellectual, and spiritual assaults of this life. People need a safe and secure shelter where they can share their problems and pleasures, give and receive forgiveness, find help, and feel loved. This doesn't happen automatically. It takes hard work and sacrifice. Building such a home will take a great deal of energy and efficiency. But can you build anything of lasting value without hard work? *Someone* has to have the time to give to this. *Someone* needs to consider the home as a career. If you are working outside your home, give as much to your job as duty requires. Do your work as unto the Lord (Ephesians 6:5–8). But remember, you are only "tent making."[8] Your first and greatest ministry is to those under your roof. Listen to Edith Schaeffer's wise words on building a home:

> In the process of providing all the economic needs of the family, if the family itself is being wiped out entirely, it all becomes a sad farce. How many people today are rationalizing the fact that they are neglecting to make any kind of home at all and failing to spend any time with their children—because they are "providing more" or "being fulfilled" or proving they are not "downtrodden slaves to a house" or "doing good works"! It is possible to destroy the family, your own and others', because your home has fallen apart in the name of "doing good works." There is a great need for *stopping* as a family together, discussing, praying, asking God, "Please show us before it is too late; what balance are we to have in our family in order to have time together before it is too late?" What is worth putting first?[9]

To be fearlessly feminine means accepting the challenge of building a shelter for those you love as your highest earthly challenge. It means submitting to the hard work, the mundane, the unglamorous. To be a fearless homemaker requires more self-motivation than a job outside your home. At least that was true for me. In my profession, I was praised for my work by parents and administrators. And if their praise waned, I still received a paycheck every two weeks. But the rewards of my family life and all that has taken place as we've talked and cried and prayed and laughed together could never even begin to compare to any paycheck or pat on the back.

If we are to devote ourselves to our homes, we must be confident that we are engaging in an eternally important and worthwhile enterprise for which God has uniquely suited us. Our motivation will come from the satisfaction of knowing that we have, by God's grace, created a smoothly running household, where needs are met, desires are respected, harmony is enjoyed, and God is lifted up.

Those voices that whisper to us, "You'll be more appreciated out there" or "Do what you want to do—it's your life" or "Go to work and hire someone to do these tasks for you" will undermine the foundation of your home and diminish your influence for godliness on those in your family. Your drive for equality and freedom and significance in others' eyes could lead you down a lonely road that ends in a secluded, forlorn, desolate cavern filled only with yourself. Somewhere along the line we must recognize our search for self-defined fulfillment as hollow and shallow.

Jesus summons us to deny ourselves and lay down our lives sacrificially for Him (Luke 9:23–25). It takes a costly investment of time, energy, thought, creativity, endurance, and selflessness to build a home of eternal significance. No wonder the woman of Proverbs 31 is clothed with strength and dignity (vv. 17, 25). She is absolutely dependable—both thrifty and industrious (v. 11), with an eye to savvy investing (vv. 16, 18). She takes great care with the running of her home (vv. 13–15, 27) and makes it a place of peace and beauty and welcome (vv. 20–21). And she does all this without whining or complaining, gently giving wise instruction to her household (v. 26). A tall order? Definitely, but *why aim for anything less?*

Transferring Truth

Not only does the fearlessly feminine woman work hard at building a home that is a shelter, she also makes her home a school, where God's truths can be passed down from one generation to another. The Scriptures admonish us to convey to our children an authentic faith:

> What we have heard and known, what our fathers have told us. We will not hide them from their children; we will tell the next generation the praiseworthy deeds of the LORD, his power, and the wonders he has done. (Psalm 78:3–4)

> Only be careful, and watch yourselves closely so that you do not forget the things your eyes have seen or let them slip from your heart as long as you live. Teach them to your children and to their children after them. (Deuteronomy 4:9)

> These commandments that I give you today are to be upon your hearts. Impress them on your children. Talk about them when you sit at home and when you walk along the road, when you lie down and when you get up. (Deuteronomy 6:6–7)

The truth of the existence and character of God must be clearly taught to our children, and the ideal place for this is in our homes. The next generation must hear from *us* the wonder of who God is, what He has said and done, and what He means to this sin-saddened world. God calls *us* to pass on His truth from one generation to another. To do this will take time and words, both planned and unplanned. As a woman you must manage your household in such a way as to give these precious eternal truths the attention they deserve. Do others see more of God because of your presence in the home? Psalm 102:28 says, "The children of your servants will live in your presence; their descendants will be established before you." Does God's presence pervade your home? Do beauty and order reign in the simple details of your everyday life as a family? Develop the art of living together, a sense of belonging, an appreciation of continuity, an awareness of *God*.

Do you sense, as I do, how time-poor and frazzled our homelife has become over the last few decades? Dinner often consists of a drive-through meal wolfed down between Boy Scouts and soccer and piano. Has your home become little more than a place to sleep and shower? Families need time together. The fearlessly feminine homemaker learns to budget her family's schedule as well as its income.

Retrieve the rich joy of sharing at least one home-cooked, nutritious, and beautifully presented, sit-down meal together each day. In our home it is dinner. Maybe breakfast would suit your schedule better. Flowers or candles, pretty placemats and matching napkins, freshly baked bread, colorful steamed vegetables or sweet fresh fruit, and a flavorful main course will soothe and satisfy your loved ones. Shared meals mean shared relationships. Ray often says that having a person in our home for a meal is worth six months of shaking hands after the church service.

Meals were a part of Jesus' ministry. Food builds a closer kind of communication. Sorrows can be shared, humor enhanced, joys celebrated, and courtesies reinforced. And then, when everyone is feeling happy and loved and pleasantly full, what a perfect time to share God's Word over a sweet dessert. How satisfying to take in His words and discuss them, passing on His truths to one another. How precious to spend time together in prayer, sharing our needs and praising God together.

Along with corporate family times, there must be opportunities for individual dialogue. Through the years, Ray has made it a point to meet with our sons alone to pray and talk and share Scripture. I discipled Krista with two other girls her age during her early teenage years, passing the truth from one generation to another. The kids always seemed more willing to open up when I offered to help them with the dishes or with one of their other chores. Around the Ping-Pong table, walking the dog, raking leaves, or cleaning up rooms, these are the unplanned times a fearlessly feminine homemaker takes advantage of to impress God's truths on her children.

Making Memories

What memories are you making in your domestic domain? Each home has its own distinct environment. Does yours speak of the Creator of the universe? Are peace and beauty and comfort and welcome to be found there? Is communication clear and kind, leaving room for criticism without allowing anyone to be crushed through cruel or angry outbursts? When hurt and resentment flare up, are there legitimate ways to express it while still keeping a guard over one's mouth (Psalm 141:3)? Can people be honest without injuring one another unfairly (Ephesians 4:25–27)?

The fearlessly feminine woman sets an example for her household to follow. She knows there are some things that must *never* be said no matter what the level of frustration or anger. What memories are being formed in the environment of your home? Children should learn kindness, compassion, and self-control at home. When they don't, schools and communities are forced to pick up the pieces of their cruel, selfish, and uncontrolled behavior.

A home must demonstrate love in the day-to-day circumstances of life: lost keys, a wet bed, spilled milk, a forgotten favor, a bruised ego. Over and over again as we express love and care and concern, we show our children how valuable they are. I am writing this chapter from bed after unexpected major surgery. Mother and Dad drove 1,100 miles to our home here in Georgia and spent two weeks nursing me and caring for my family. They cleaned and did laundry; they carpooled and cooked; they gardened and watered plants indoors and out; they shopped and ran errands. And in between all that, they sat with me and helped pass the hours until I was well enough to get up. What a treat it was to hear one of them climbing the stairs with a fresh tray of food, ice cubes tinkling in some delicious fruit drink. Each gesture said, "We love you, Jani. We value you. We care deeply about your well-being. How can we help you?"

So, how are you showing the love of God to those around you? Don't make your home just another item on your "to do" list. God calls you to devote yourself to your home above any career. If you are too busy to manage it well, who will do it?

Are you building a stable home or are you tearing yours down? Someone needs to have the vision for creating an atmosphere where faith and obedience can be nurtured, for developing an environment where love and security are readily accessible. This takes time. You must be there for the teachable moments. You must cultivate a setting where family members can thrive and grow, memories can be built, fears comforted, convictions formed, and needs met in ways that are impossible in any other setting than a home.

> *Home to laughter, home to rest,*
> *Home to those we love the best...*
> *Now the day is done and I*
> *Turn to hear a welcoming cry.*
> *Love is dancing at the door,*
> *And I am safe at home once more.*[10]

Channel your energies and imagination and skills into the most meaningful work in the world: managing your household, creating a shelter, and developing a center for truth to be passed on to the next generation. Multiply your legacy by being fearlessly devoted to the affairs of your household.

Study Questions

1. Imagine it is your eighty-fifth birthday. Friends and family are gathered to help you celebrate. What would you most like to see and hear to make it a meaningful celebration?

2. Who and what receive the most productive hours and freshest energies of your days? How can you adjust your commitments so that your family receives the best that you can give them?

3. In what area is it hardest for you to surrender to your call as a woman? Why? How can you trust God with that struggle?

4. List the relationships in your home. What can you do to ensure that needs are met, desires respected, and harmony enjoyed by all who enter your door?

5. How can you use your home to show God to those around you? Who of the next generation are you training for the years ahead?

She opens her arms to the poor and
extends her hands to the needy.

<small>PROVERBS 31:20</small>

Saved to Serve
AMY CARMICHAEL
(1867–1951)

I n 1895, Amy Carmichael arrived in India as a single missionary, dangerously ill with dengue fever. She was no
stranger to serious illness. Indeed, she had suffered other
life-threatening ailments during her work in Japan, China, and
Ceylon. Her deep spiritual passion gave her no choice but to
ride this wave, as she had many others, without letting it over-
take her, despite the urgings of well-meaning friends in Britain
who implored her to return to her homeland.

For the next fifty-three years Amy was to serve her Master
in India without a furlough. She founded the Dohnavur
Fellowship as a refuge for children who otherwise would have
become temple prostitutes. Hers is the story of a steadfast, disciplined woman who maintained exhaustingly high standards
for herself and her fellowship members. She was utterly single-
hearted, thoroughly consumed with the life of obedience to the
things of God. Her life was that of a soldier following her
Captain. "Saved to serve" was a motto those around her saw
her live out. She once wrote back to London, "To any whom
the Divine Hand is beckoning: count the cost, for He tells us
to, *but take your slate to the foot of the Cross and add up the figures
there.*"[1]

Amy had an acutely sensitive nature and was endowed
with unusual gifts, especially literary talents. Her letters and
books illuminate for us a life of sacrifice, serving the Light of
the World in the midst of the darkness of sin's opposition,
bereavement, and physical deprivation.

She taught the children God brought to her to value truth,

courage, and self-control, telling them, "Be the first wherever there is a sacrifice to be made, a self-denial to be practiced, or an impetus to be given."[2] And her own life made these truths visible to them all. She devoted her whole self to the sole purpose of eternal things. The year that her mother died found Amy nursing her trusted helper, Ponnammal, through two operations while she herself suffered from neuralgia. At the same time 70 out of the 140 children living at Dohnavur came down with malaria. How could she go on? In her quest for uncompromising obedience and a pure knowledge of God, she wrote this prayer:

> And shall I pray Thee change Thy will, my Father,
> Until it be according unto mine?
> But, no, Lord, no, that never shall be, rather
> I pray Thee blend my human will with Thine.[3]

She had asked God to free her from "silken self...easy choices, weakenings." Amy Carmichael's commitment to take up her cross and follow the way of the crucified Lord meant death to herself in all shapes and forms. Her life was a blending of her will with God's.

CHAPTER EIGHT

Confidently Caring for Others

We women offer something to our culture that only feminine souls can contribute. Women have an extraordinary capacity for comforting others that arises from our uniquely feminine response toward those around us. Our nurturing instincts bring sensitivity, courage, and warmth to relationships. Think of how dry and barren our homes, our churches, and our communities would be without any feminine presence. Society needs us.

If the spotlight of public attention that has shone on women over the past thirty years were to be turned in your direction, what would it reveal? What characterizes your life? On what is your emotional energy focused? For many, our actions revolve around ourselves and our private welfare. But Christian women are to have God's plans and purposes as the center of their lives. We are to live to please Him. And we please Him by living lives of compassion, mercy, and personal sacrifice.

God's Creative Design for Us

The highest call of the feminine soul is to give and nurture life throughout all its various stages. Many women do this physically, and we honor them. But not all women are called to give biological birth. Every Christian woman *is* called, however, to participate in the spiritual birth and nurturing of others around her. If you don't know someone who needs your mercy and kindness in the name of Christ, then you are missing out on a wonderful part of God's plan for you. The fearlessly feminine woman does not live in isolation, indifferent and aloof. She is involved. She is sensitive to those around her, eager to meet their needs.

The God who is "rich in mercy" (Ephesians 2:4) calls us to respond with fearless femininity to human needs. How we treat others shows what our lives are really made of. Our good deeds are a living theology for those with whom we rub shoulders. We who have received so much from God must confidently share His kindness with others. A woman of Christlike kindness has been refreshed at God's spring of generosity and has experienced His expansive goodness. Her deeds of mercy are a display of her relationship with God. It is the gospel that motivates and energizes her to reach out to others. When God pours out His lovingkindness into a woman's sinful heart, her response is to reach out to others with that same lovingkindness. As C. S. Lewis explains:

> That is why the Christian is in a different position from other people who are trying to be good. They hope, by being good, to please God if there is one; or—if they think there is not—at least they hope to deserve approval from good men. But the Christian thinks any

good he does comes from the Christ-life inside him. He does not think God will love us because we are good, but that God will make us good because He loves us.[4]

A fearlessly feminine woman never counts on good works to win her favor with God. She understands that she can bring nothing to the bargaining table to make herself impressive in God's eyes. Her heavenly Father and His Son have settled her account at the cross without any help from her. But precisely because God has won her heart, drawing her near to Himself through the death of His Son (Ephesians 2:13), her love for God spills over into acts of service and love for others (Ephesians 5:1–2). Her life makes credible and beautiful the gospel that has captured her soul: "These good works…are the fruits and evidences of a true and lively faith."[5]

The wonderful thing about acts of kindness and deeds of mercy is that through them we can show others what Christ is like. Jesus fed the hungry, taught the ignorant, healed the sick, and touched the untouchable. Not only did He teach us by example, but also by word. He calls us to live lives of mercy, despite the inconvenience and hassle. Think of the story of the Good Samaritan. Jesus tells us to "Go and do likewise" (Luke 10:37). Whom has God placed on your daily path with needs for protection, money, shelter, or food—both literal and spiritual? When we reach out to the sick or hungry, the poor or needy, the hurting or lonely, we are to do it as if we were doing it for Christ Himself (Matthew 25:35–40). Open your eyes to the needy around you. Serve Christ by serving them. Do you want your neighbor or coworker or child or parent to be attracted to Christ? Then show him or her what Christ is like through a Christlike life.

This way of living is God's will for us. Ephesians 2:10 says that we were "created in Christ Jesus to do good works, which God prepared in advance for us to do." As you show His kindness and mercy to others, you are fulfilling one of God's great creative designs for you as His daughter. Do you ever wonder about God's will for your life? Start with the good works He has laid on your heart or brought to your door. He created you for them.

Where to Begin

Where should we begin? What should be the first step in reaching out in kindness to others? God says it should begin in His church: "Let us not become weary in doing good, for at the proper time we will reap a harvest if we do not give up. Therefore, as we have opportunity, let us do good to all people, especially to those who belong to the family of believers" (Galatians 6:9–10).

How precious is our family of believers—and how needy! So often we think of "good works" as foreign missions trips or soup kitchens for the homeless or projects to combat world hunger or other valid efforts "out there." These are good, but they are not where we begin. We ought to be *especially* alert to the family of believers. In this world of pain and loneliness we must care about one another. Mercy and kindness ought to start in our own homes and then spread to our small groups and our Sunday school classes and others in our church and then, finally, embrace those outside the family of believers. It is tempting to overlook those nearest to us in our efforts to do good.

Tenderness and good deeds ought to begin at home with your husband and your children. What needs for love and kindness are they expressing to you? Are you making an effort to hear them? Are you sensitive to these needs, or are you too busy with details and dinners and diapers to respond to their appeals for your loving attention? It is often hardest to show thoughtful sensitivity to your children. Don't be afraid that a little extra TLC might pamper or spoil them. We may feel somewhat guilty if we digress from our strict code of obedience and respect. But when we concentrate only on building character and independence, we miss some of the joys that little deeds of kindness bring. And doesn't love, too, build character? Allow yourself the freedom to treat your children as you would want to be treated if you found yourself in their shoes. Let them taste the comfort of the Golden Rule within their own home before you ask them to demonstrate it to others.

It was hot yesterday when I stepped out to do some errands—I mean Georgia-in-July hot! Gavin, sixteen, was getting on his bike to ride over to a friend's. I offered him a ride, which for our family was unusual since this friend lives only a short distance away. Gavin was grateful, and in just the few minutes we had together, he opened up to share a personal prayer request with me. It was a precious moment between mother and teenage son, flowing from a small deed of kindness.

Lighting a Dark and Troubled World

Beyond the walls of your home, to whom are you reaching out? God calls us to let our deeds of kindness spill over into the world around us. Peter admonishes, "Live such good lives among the pagans that, though they accuse you of doing wrong, *they may see your good deeds* and glorify God on the day he visits us" (1 Peter 2:12, italics mine). And Jesus says, "You are the light of the world. A city on a hill cannot be hidden.

Neither do people light a lamp and put it under a bowl. Instead they put it on its stand, and it gives light to everyone in the house. In the same way, let your light shine before men, *that they may see your good deeds* and praise your Father in heaven" (Matthew 5:14–16, italics mine). Our "good deeds" should be clearly evident to those around us, a light in this dark and troubled world for those who haven't yet tasted God's grace. Only women who have freely received God's mercy in their own lives can give it to others without looking for recognition or reward. The fearlessly feminine woman should be known for her good deeds.

While I was writing this chapter, Hurricane Floyd began battering the coast of Georgia and the Carolinas, sending thousands to seek shelter here in Augusta. When one of our staff realized that there were six hundred people camping out at the civic center next door to our church, she wondered how she could help. Food was their main concern, as the influx of evacuees was taxing our restaurants and some food supplies. So, ever efficient and caring, Patti spent her day shopping and organizing and calling. Sandwiches were made and delivered, and many evening and predawn hours were spent preparing warm breakfasts for the hundreds who were far from home and worried about what would be left when they returned. Patti will receive little earthly recognition for her exhausting effort. Nor does she seek any. She did it because she has tasted God's mercy herself and longs to be a light in the darkness of this present age.

Trained by Veterans

Paul taught that a woman's life should be characterized by her compassion for others. When he was writing to Timothy about how the church should care for its widows, good deeds appeared prominently in the qualifications for women who should receive support from the church (1 Timothy 5:9–10). Apparently there was a list of women in need of some sort of financial aid, and to be placed on it, a widow had to be "well known for her good deeds, such as bringing up children, showing hospitality, washing the feet of the saints, helping those in trouble and devoting herself to all kinds of good deeds" (v. 10).

The church should honor women who have spent themselves for others. The Bible considers bringing up children (the most helpless and vulnerable and guileless among us) a good deed that should be honored as a woman gets older. She also must be hospitable, opening her home and heart to those who need shelter, food, and a warm welcome. She should be a woman who humbly cares for the personal comforts of others ("washing the feet of the saints") and a merciful helper to "those in trouble." She must be sensitive, hard working, dedicated "to all kinds of good deeds." What a woman! Her life testifies loving servanthood to any and all. She has earned the grateful care of the church.

No wonder Paul writes to Titus that one of the responsibilities of the older women in the church is to train the younger women to be kind (Titus 2:5). This way of living does not naturally spring out of our self-centered hearts. Not only do we need to be born again by the Spirit of God, we also need to be trained and encouraged by veterans who know what it means to confidently care for others.

Perhaps you have been fortunate, as I have, to see this kind of woman in action. Jeline was our pastor's wife while we lived in Illinois. I saw her work tirelessly, serving her family, her kindergarten students, her church, and her neighbors. Her dining table often had guests around it. One question her children grew up asking every Sunday morning was, "Who is coming for dinner *today?*"

Whenever I was under the weather, I would get a call that Jeline was dropping a meal off. She cheerfully gave up her Sunday morning worship times to minister to the children of our church. Though she never let on to me, I knew she would have loved to have worshiped with the adults and heard her husband, Kent, preach. When friends had a court date or a difficult doctor's appointment or a flooded basement, she was there, offering support and comfort. She served in women's ministries at both local and state levels in our denomination. She always found time to talk to those who needed her wise counsel.

Even now that hundreds of miles separate us, I still hear about her good deeds through our eldest son, Eric, who is on Kent's staff as youth pastor. Eric often is in their home sharing a meal, discussing a good book, or playing family games with these servants of God. And guess who gave him rides recently when his car broke down?

Perhaps you haven't been privileged with a close-up example of a caring, older woman. Then turn to God's Word for help. Don't shortchange the Bible. In it you will find all that you need to become a fearlessly feminine, confidently caring woman. Come before God and, through His Word, expose your soul to Him. Ask Him where He wants you to reach out to others in mercy and kindness. Paul wrote in 2 Timothy 3:16–17, "All Scripture is God-breathed and is useful for teaching, rebuking, correcting and training in righteousness, so that the man [or woman] of God may be thoroughly equipped for every good work." Come to His Word. Study it daily. He will shape you. He will show you how to fulfill this aspect of His call for you as His daughter. "And God is able to make all grace abound to you, so that in all things at all times, having all that you need, you will abound in every good work" (2 Corinthians 9:8). Through His grace, you will have what you need to do God's will. In every way, at all times, God will help you overflow with good works.

The God Who Remembers

Before we turn our attention to practical suggestions, let's consider one more facet of deeds of mercy and kindness. We must never confuse good works with a works righteousness. God does not owe us anything for doing the good works He created us to do, yet they are pleasing and acceptable to Him through the cleansing blood of Christ. They demonstrate the authenticity of our faith in Jesus Christ. His grace frees us to follow Jesus. For Jesus' sake, God accepts and rewards that which is imperfect, but sincere. Hebrews 13:15–16 tells us, "Through Jesus, therefore, let us continually offer to God a sacrifice of praise— the fruit of lips that confess his name. And do not forget to do good and to share with others, for with such sacrifices God is pleased." And we have the encouragement that "you come to the help of those who gladly do right" (Isaiah 64:5). Good works are God's will for us. They are also the pathway of His blessing for us. Let's embrace them confidently!

Jesus taught that in our lives of service, we should take the attitude of unworthy servants who are only doing our duty (Luke 17:10). If that were all He told us about caring for others, we might grow weary or disheartened. But God promises that He is no man's debtor. "God is not unjust; he will not forget your work and the love you have shown him as you have helped his people and continue to help them" (Hebrews 6:10). He is the God who *remembers*. He counts any help you give to others along the way as love shown directly to Him. And in His justice, He will remember your efforts. He tells us that those who are rich in good deeds, generous, and willing to share are laying up a treasure for themselves in the coming age (1 Timothy 6:18–19). He takes your good deeds and invests them in a heavenly account assigned to you. The fearlessly feminine woman makes generous deposits to her eternal account. She is a happy servant of Jesus. She is free to give herself unstintingly to others because she is loved by the God who remembers.

A Starting Point

I would like to end this chapter with some practical tips on how to help those in need around you. It is just a beginning. I hope you'll add your own ideas to this list. There are as many good works as there are needs to be met. Here are some suggestions to get you started:

- Prepare and deliver a meal in disposable containers.
- Offer to organize meals and errands if there is a need for extended care.
- Drop off a basket of fresh fruit.
- Send note cards, pens, and stamps.
- Bring fresh flowers or a plant.
- Share a book you have enjoyed, either to borrow or to keep.
- Create homemade coupons to be redeemed for errand running.

- Volunteer a few hours of housekeeping or gardening. Bring your own mop or hoe.
- Send a card, sharing a happy memory or an uplifting verse that can be tucked away to be read over and over.
- Offer rides to the doctor or lawyer or airport or beauty shop. (Our family is so grateful to the lady who brings my ninety-seven-year-old grandmother home every Friday from her hair appointment.)
- Offer to baby-sit or parent-sit.
- Create a "pamper yourself" basket full of items such as bubble bath, scented lotion, chocolate truffles, and fruit teas.
- Come with supplies needed to give your friend a manicure and/or a pedicure.
- Older people love a visit. Just go and chat for a while.
- Sometimes troubled teens need other adults in their lives to talk with and cheer them on. A lunch date or your presence at one of their special events can go a long way to help them through rough waters.
- Start a collection for a friend: thimbles, teapots, birdhouses, baskets, spoons. It can become a treasury of shared memories through the years.
- Walk once a week with someone who needs exercise or a listening ear or a change of scenery.
- Organize a marriage retreat for a couple who needs time together. Your part could range from watching their children to actually treating them to one or two nights away.
- Open a spare room in your house for someone who needs safety or renewal or rest.
- Prepare a bag full of paper goods to help alleviate kitchen cleanup during times of trials or illness.

The list could go on and on. Who can you help on the way to heaven with your confidently caring fearless femininity? Who needs your offering of kindness and mercy? God loves us in our needs, not for our virtues. We in turn should love the needy. Love much because you are much loved. Your sacrifices of compassion and mercy will seem light because they will be lightened by love.

Be Strong

Be strong!
We are not here to play, to dream, to drift;
We have hard work to do, and loads to lift:
Shun not the struggle—face it; 'tis God's gift.

Be strong!
Say not, "The days are evil. Who's to blame?"
And fold the hands and acquiesce—oh shame!
Stand up, speak out, and bravely, in God's name.

Be strong!
It matters not how deep intrenched the wrong
How hard the battle goes, the day how long;
Faint not—fight on! To-morrow comes the song.
MALTBIE D. BABCOCK (1858–1901)[6]

Be strong! You are so loved by God. Give yourself to others, and your life will be fearlessly feminine.

Study Questions

1. Read 1 Timothy 2:9–10. In what sense can a woman "dress" herself with good deeds?

2. When you have needed compassion and kindness, what did people do for you that was helpful? Unhelpful?

3. What can you add to the list of ideas for mercy and kindness in this chapter?

4. What evidences are there in your life of a true and lively faith (James 2:18, 22)?

5. Read Hebrews 13:16. What sacrifices of goodness and generosity is God asking you to offer to Him?

Grace was in all her steps, heaven in her eye,
In every gesture dignity and love.

JOHN MILTON

The Only Godly Fear
SARAH EDWARDS
?–1758

I
t was after one of evangelist George Whitefield's visits to the home of Jonathan and Sarah Edwards that he wrote of Sarah, "She is a woman adorn'd with a meek and quiet spirit; [she] talked feelingly and solidly of the things of God, and seemed to be such a helpmeet for her husband, that she caused me to renew those prayers which, for months I have put up to God, that he should be pleased to send me a daughter of Abraham to be my wife."[1]

Sarah was known for her piety, gentleness, and graciousness. The American Indians, among whom she and her family lived from 1750–1758, loved her quiet temperament. She was intensely loyal, strong, and dignified, and greatly loved by her husband and their eleven children. She was never known to raise her voice during her busy days, yet she allowed no disrespect from her brood. Her children learned obedience under her firm, quiet manner, as she taught them all the useful pioneer duties.

Sarah was a woman of amazing serenity, even in the midst of Indian attacks, life-threatening diseases, and the rigors of feeding and clothing a large family in such primitive conditions. Her husband once recorded in his journal that when their home had to be converted into a fort to protect the twelve settler families in the small settlement of Stockbridge, Sarah served 180 meals for builders and 800 meals for fleeing refugees.

In the midst of all her busyness, she maintained a quiet heart before God. She was His daughter and she walked like a child with Him through both the hardships and happinesses of her frontier life. As one biographer put it, "She knew with the wisdom of the years that the only godly fear was for the 'frowns of God.'"[2]

CHAPTER NINE

Unfading Beauty

What makes a woman beautiful? Who sets the standards for our definition of beauty? Is it Hollywood and beauty pageant judges? Why does one person excite our senses and bring us more aesthetic satisfaction than another?

Beauty is hard to define. If someone were to ask you, "Who would you describe as a beautiful woman?" you would probably think of some well-known woman who might fit a generally accepted cultural image of beauty. But if you were asked what actually makes her beautiful, you might struggle for words to explain why you chose her. Beauty is hard to define, but it is a universal quality that fascinates us all.

A few years ago, our daughter, Krista, and I were extras in a Julia Roberts film that was being shot at an historic mansion in our town. The film crew needed about three hundred locals to participate in various scenes, and Krista and I signed up. The filming lasted all night long for several nights. We stayed in a big warehouse, waiting and reading and visiting with the other extras from around 7:00 P.M. to 5:00 A.M. It was hot. It was boring. Finally, they bussed several of us to the set where we were to act as wedding guests of Julia's friend who was getting married. It took about two hours to place us all in our various spots and give us instructions. When the director was finally ready to start filming, Julia's stand-in left, and everyone strained to get a look as the real Julia Roberts walked onto the set.

She was beautiful. What other word could describe her? I found myself struck at how she carried herself with a natural grace. We couldn't help but stare. Her skin, her eyes, her hair, her smile were combined in such a pleasing way that we all simply enjoyed watching her. I don't think this was entirely due to all the Hollywood hype that surrounds young actresses today. There was something in each one of our definitions of *beautiful* that Julia Roberts fit, though those definitions varied from person to person.

The Beauty of Inner Serenity

What is God's definition of beauty? He is the one who created it. What does *He* find beautiful in a woman? The Bible tells the stories of stunningly beautiful women: Sarah, Rebecca, Rachel, Bathsheba, Abigail, Esther, and others. God made us creatures who enjoy beauty, and that beauty finds a place in His Word. He wired us together in such a way that the beauty seen in His creative works releases in us an irrepressible admiration. The radiance of beautiful people and things catches our eye. It holds our attention. We were made to be attracted to beauty. It delights and satisfies us.

But God cautions us not to elevate beauty above its proper place. He warns us in Proverbs 31:30 that "beauty is fleeting." It does not endure. It is transitory. Perhaps it is the ephemeral nature of beauty that prompts us to admire it so avidly. It is hard to capture, easy to lose, and impossible to retain for long. We know beauty won't last forever, so we seek to enjoy it to the fullest whenever it appears.

God gives us His definition of a beautiful woman in 1 Peter 3. The Bible affirms a beauty that reaches beyond our human definitions. This kind of beauty surpasses what earthbound eyes can see. To be fearlessly feminine, a woman must genuinely embrace God's description of true beauty. It is a beauty that no cosmetic or wardrobe or diet can enhance. Peter describes what God finds beautiful in His daughters in 1 Peter 3:3–4: "Your beauty should not come from outward adornment, such as braided hair and the wearing of gold jewelry and fine clothes. Instead, it should be that of your inner self, the unfading beauty of a gentle and quiet spirit, which is of great worth in God's sight."

There is an unfading beauty that a woman can develop that is precious to God. It is a costly beauty, "of great worth in God's sight." It is a lasting beauty. It will never evanesce. Notice the adjective *unfading*. This word can be translated *indestructible, incorruptible, imperishable,* hence, *immortal.* It speaks of a beauty that is damage resistant, incapable of being destroyed, not subject to decay or death—in other words, everlasting. There is a beauty that wrinkles cannot diminish, age cannot dim, and death cannot destroy. God is the judge of this kind of beauty, and His judgment is sincere and heartfelt. He has true and lasting beauty for you and for me. Does that thrill you as it does me? This inner beauty is powerful, pure, and permanent. And it is precious in the sight of God.

There is a beauty that the fearlessly feminine woman can, by God's grace, cultivate here on earth and take with her into heaven. It is the everlasting beauty of "a gentle and quiet spirit." God is calling us out of our troubled turbulence into an unruffled inner ease that will be as welcome in heaven as it is valuable here on earth.

Why is a gentle and quiet spirit pleasing to God? Because serenity is a sign of trust. When we are agitated and restless, we are responding to life in fear. Worry leaves no room for God's way to be trusted. What enables us to be gentle and quiet in the hidden part of our feminine souls? What produces an inner serenity in the midst of tumult? It is a deep confidence in God's loving care, in His Fatherly protection. It is the belief that He holds only the kindest intentions toward us.

In 1 Samuel 25 we are told the story of Abigail, a beautiful woman who revealed an imperturbable spirit in the midst of chaos. Abigail was married to a churlish fool. Nabal was "surly and mean in his dealings" (v. 3). Yet Abigail remained sensitive and beautiful even when she was surrounded with crudeness. When David asked Nabal to return a favor, Nabal's insulting and ungrateful response angered him so much that he called his men to arms. Disaster was hanging over Nabal and his whole household (v. 17). Who did Nabal's servants turn to for help in this alarming situation? The intelligent and beautiful Abigail (vv. 14–17). She saw the need for a speedy response to avert almost certain bloodshed. So she prepared a generous gift to appease David's injured pride and regain his goodwill toward her household.

Abigail demonstrates that a gentle and quiet spirit does not mean being passive or inert. She used her intelligence without being rude or pushy. She acted quickly, yet without harshness or agitation (vv. 18–19). She understood that God was in control, and she spoke words of wisdom from a gentle and quiet heart (v. 30). She portrayed a regal dignity that reflected the serenity of her inner being, despite the surrounding turmoil. Abigail did not let fear rule her heart, and God esteems a woman like that.

Within your own heart today there are seeds of beauty that can bear fruit. Your trust in God will water them. As you walk with Him in faith and obedience, these seeds will blossom into an imperishable beauty that you can take all the way into heaven with you. Don't let the cares of this world mar the beauty that God wants to develop in you, His daughter. Guard your heart of all that would rob you of contentment. Spend your lifetime beautifying yourself for heaven. Tend to that which will be yours throughout eternity—the unfading beauty of a gentle and quiet spirit.

The Beauty of Purity

Another beauty of the fearlessly feminine woman is purity. Peter speaks of purity—that careful correctness of behavior that gives a woman a certain innocence as well as a developed integrity—in the verses immediately preceding his teaching on the beauty of a gentle and quiet spirit. "Wives, in the same way be submissive to your husbands so that, if any of them do not believe the word, they may be won over without words by the behavior of their wives, when they see the purity and reverence of your lives" (1 Peter 3:1–2).

As Christian women, we must understand God's holiness and purity and our own desperate need to be cleansed if we are to stand in His presence. In the Old Testament, from the Israelites' meeting with God at Mount Sinai (Exodus 19) to Josiah purifying the land (2 Chronicles 34), we see God requiring purity in order for His people to approach Him. And now, in the New Testament, the pure righteousness of His Son, Jesus Christ, has been credited to all those who believe on Him (Romans 3:21–26). Christ has paid the price to cleanse us and make us fit to commune with a holy God. The fearlessly feminine woman has been freed from the guilt of her sin. She is no longer intimidated by her past. She responds to God's grace in gratitude by consecrating herself to an upright life, pleasing to her Father.

God's mercy motivates us to live lives of personal purity. In Romans 12:1, Paul makes an appeal to us: "Therefore, I urge you, brothers, in view of God's mercy, to offer your bodies as living sacrifices, holy and pleasing to God—this is your spiritual act of worship." On what does Paul base his appeal? On the basis of God's *mercy.* Does God seem merciful to you? Does His mercy move you? Have you personally tasted His mercy, or is it some nebulous doctrine that makes you yawn?

There are many reasons why we might be strangers to God's mercy. Here are just a few:

God's mercy is often unseen. Stop and think for a minute of all the stories of close calls you've heard or read about. Some would call these luck or fate. But the Bible teaches that God orders all things (Proverbs 16:33). God in His mercy protects and surrounds us (Psalm 91:11, 14). We will probably never fully realize the extent of His loving mercies toward us, for His compassion and patience are often hidden in all our daily comings and goings. If only we had eyes to *see* His mercy!

God's mercy is not fully understood. We don't fully comprehend God's mercy. This is especially true of His supreme act of mercy, the Cross. The sacrifice of His only Son, blameless and perfect, to make a way for us sinners to commune with Him, should fill us with wonder. But sometimes this doesn't seem enough for us. We keep looking for more tangible signs of His love and mercy, when He has already given us the ultimate. If only we had minds to *comprehend* His mercy!

God's mercy is unappreciated. When God's mercy doesn't fit *our* definition of mercy, we become frustrated and angry with Him. We lose our fear and awe of God. We "un-god" Him by passing judgment on Him for not measuring up to our expectations of what God should be like. If only we had hearts to *revere* His mercy!

If we aren't tasting God's mercy, it isn't God's fault. The fault lies in our blind, ignorant, and arrogant hearts. Listen to how God is described in His Word. He is:

- the Father of compassion (2 Corinthians 1:3);
- the loving God who is rich in mercy (Ephesians 2:4);
- the understanding Father who cares for us as a father does his children (Psalm 103:13–14);
- the gracious, blameless, compassionate Protector of those in need (Psalm 12:5);
- the One who sympathizes with our physical needs (Matthew 15:32);

- the One who has compassion for our emotional needs (Matthew 9:36);
- the God of tender reunions (Luke 15:20).

Ask God to soften your heart toward His mercies. Then your obedience will be a cheerful sacrifice of gratitude. When, in Romans 12:1, Paul urges us to *offer* our bodies to God, he uses a verb that hints at a willing dedication, the way a bride presents herself to her bridegroom. Our cheerful willingness emerges from hearts that have been overwhelmed by the love of our Father.

Notice that Paul tells us to offer our *bodies*. We are not to obey the desires of our bodies that displease God. We are called as Christians to honor God with our very bodies (Romans 6:12; 1 Corinthians 6:20; and 2 Corinthians 5:9–10). The unfading beauty of a pure woman is not easily or quickly developed. It takes both physical and spiritual consecration. The sacrifice of purity will be costly; it always costs something to follow God.

God has given us a comprehensive view of who He is and what He expects of us throughout all of Scripture. He Himself is our pattern. We are to be holy and like Him (1 Peter 1:15–16). How? "Let us purify ourselves from everything that contaminates body and spirit, perfecting holiness out of reverence for God" (2 Corinthians 7:1). What compromises your purity in God's sight?

- bitter thoughts?
- anger or resentment?
- self-pitying homesickness?
- diet excesses (either too much or too little)?

- exercise obsessions?
- questionable TV shows or videos?
- fantasies that you feed?

God is asking us to offer our bodies to Him as living sacrifices that are "holy and pleasing" to Him. The fearlessly feminine woman understands that this calls for a conscious, intelligent, consecrated devotion to the beauty of personal purity. This doesn't mean that God expects sinless perfection. But He does look for a single-mindedness (James 4:8), an unmixed devotion (Psalm 24:4), a wholehearted seeking of His face (Psalm 119:58). Where are the women who will give themselves wholly to God? No more divided loyalties, no more double standards, no more secret idols?

God is holy and pure, and He expects His character to be reflected in His daughters. In Titus 2:5 the older women are exhorted to train the younger women to be "self-controlled and pure." It is interesting that self-control and purity are closely linked. The opposite of self-control is self-indulgence. We are encouraged by our toxic popular culture to cater to our desires for food and ease, to appease our physical longings at every whim, and to coddle our bent toward gratification. But God calls us to the beauty of self-control.

The fearlessly feminine woman says no to many of her immediate desires in order to inherit the beauty that is truly desirable. She is careful to be above reproach for the sake of her Father. His grace teaches her "to say 'No' to ungodliness and worldly passions, and to live self-controlled, upright and godly lives in this present age" (Titus 2:11–12). She knows that God, through Christ, "gave himself for us to redeem us from all wickedness and to purify for himself a people that are his very own, eager to do what is good" (Titus 2:13–14).

How eager are you to do good? Is there some form of ungodliness that muddies your purity? A book? A soap opera? An impure relationship? Indiscriminate entertainment? What worldly passions mar your beauty? The desire for attention or wealth or power? The fearlessly feminine woman is not afraid to tell herself no!

What indulgences are undermining your purity? The fruit of God's Spirit includes "self-control" (Galatians 5:22–23). God is able to fill us so full of Himself that we don't even *want* to go back to the fridge over and over if those snacks are a way to find the comfort which *God* should be supplying us instead.

How will you open your heart more widely to God's Spirit? Will you indulge yourself with Him? If you do, your purity will be God beautified. It is through His grace that we can win the battle for spiritual purity.

The fearlessly feminine woman desires that God search her heart (Psalm 139:23–24). She longs for His cleansing renewal in her spirit (Psalm 51:10). She guards her purity by living according to His Word (Psalm 119:9). Her gentle and quiet spirit is a wonderful blend of gratitude for Christ's purifying work on the cross for her, and a Spirit-filled endeavor to lead a beautiful life of purity in body and spirit.

The Beauty of Modesty

Along with purity and self-control, the woman beautified with a gentle and quiet spirit is modest. Beauty is always attractive, whether it is inner or outer beauty. But to be fearlessly feminine means to draw others to ourselves because of our godly character rather than our physical attractiveness and outer finery. God can give us true beauty in our spirits that outclasses external adornments (1 Peter 3:3–6).

Your appearance will reflect what you are cultivating in your heart. What motivates you to dress and act a certain way? What is the intent of your heart? Do you want to flaunt your figure or your wealth? Do you want to use your feminine flare to call attention to yourself? A godly woman understands the importance of modesty. She knows that a man's admiration can soon turn to lust if she is careless about how she dresses and acts. Admiration and lust are not entirely exclusive, but why tip the scale to the side of lust by overexposure? Why become an object of temptation?

We live in a day of exhibitionism. It confronts us in our movies and our magazine stands. It even saturates our malls with life-sized poster advertisements of amply-endowed models wearing the latest in ladies' lingerie.

Ray and I have close friends who are devoted to raising their four young sons to be godly young men. Recently we were window shopping together. As we passed a store with posters of young beauties modeling only underpants, their six-year-old said, "Those ladies don't have enough clothes on, do they, Mommie?" It was a scene straight out of *The Emperor's New Clothes,* where a child brings into focus our foolishness. It took a child's eyes to see the obvious and a child's innocence to say it.

Our family enjoyed watching the Women's World Soccer Championship recently. But when a U.S. team member tore off her shirt in celebration of the U.S. team's victory, she did nothing but demean the occasion and disappoint her fans. Some viewers may have thought, "Umm, nice sports bra." But others were doubtless hurrying to change the channel for the sake of their thirteen-year-old son, who suddenly found the victory celebration riveting. As Mona Charen commented in a recent newspaper column:

> The usual stupid people said, "Well, the men do it." Memo to commentators: Men don't have breasts. You can look it up. If men tore off their shorts as a victory gesture and ran around in jock straps, that would be more comparable to what Chastain did. And people would think they were ridiculous. Perhaps Chastain has a need to exhibit herself. But once again, her display introduced sex where it doesn't belong.[3]

The beauty of modesty requires discretion. It also requires an understanding of how men view women and a ready acceptance of our responsibility to support them in their own attempt to be pure in their behavior toward *us*.

A woman of good taste can adapt to her culture without displeasing her Father. She knows that her body is a work of fine art, and she displays it as such—with just the right exposure. Her beauty does not evoke shock, embarrassment, or disgust. As Proverbs tell us, "Like gold in a pig's snout is a beautiful woman who shows no discretion" (Proverbs 11:22).

Our daughter, Krista, is a beautiful young woman. But more importantly, she exercises modesty and discretion. When we were working as extras in the Julia Roberts film I mentioned earlier, the wardrobe designer instructed Krista to put on a dress for a certain scene. She did and came back and told him that she wouldn't be able to wear it. It was far too revealing. With a scowl, he tossed her another dress and told her to put on that one. She did and once again came back and told him she couldn't wear it for the same reason.

Soon all three hundred extras in the room were listening to him berate Krista at the top of his lungs, asking her if she knew who he was. He yelled at her to leave immediately if she wasn't willing to wear what he chose. By then I was near her and saw her make her choice. As we gathered our things to head home, he calmed down and had one of his assistants bring Krista a beautiful, but less revealing, floor-length gown. She looked stunning in it. I was very proud of her—primarily because of her inner resolve not to flaunt her beauty. She showed fearless femininity in exercising discretion.

Many extras asked her how she could stand up to this Oscar-winning wardrobe designer, and Krista was able to share with them her commitment to lead a life that was honoring to Christ. It led to many fruitful discussions during our brief exposure to "glamorous" Hollywood.

The Bible never encourages us, however, to look dowdy. When Peter tells us how *not* to dress, he is talking about a heart attitude. "Your beauty should not come from outward adornment, such as braided hair and the wearing of gold jewelry and fine clothes. Instead, it should be that of your inner self..." (1 Peter 3:3–4). John MacArthur Jr. helps us gain insight into this passage in his book, *Different by Design:*

> In Roman society women were continually preoccupied with their external appearance. They dyed their hair outlandish colors, braided it elaborately, and were fond of expensive jewelry, elegant clothing, and fine cosmetics. Certainly Peter wasn't forbidding women from styling their hair or wearing jewelry or nice clothing;

he just didn't want them to be preoccupied with those things.[4]

We may be tempted at times to overemphasize God's warning to us. He highly values the inner beauty of godliness. But we never see in Scripture any excuse for slovenliness. How can we be winsome to those around us if we look as if we didn't care about our outward appearance? Then we might become a distraction rather than a magnet to Christ. Careless, shoddy dressing can attract just as much attention to our outward appearance as overdoing it can.

Our outward appearance should reflect the beauty and grace of true womanhood. It should show a sensitivity to the temptations the men around us face. It should demonstrate a love and commitment to our husbands. It should reveal an unmixed commitment to Christ. There must be no more ambiguity about whom we serve. We should radiate the unfading inner beauty, purity, and modesty that God is developing in those who dare to be fearlessly feminine.

Study Questions

1. Describe what God finds beautiful in a woman.

2. Read Titus 2:11–12. To what ungodliness and worldly passions are you saying yes?

3. What can you see in your life that may be impure or displeasing to your Father? What hinders and entangles you? (Hebrews 12:1). What contaminates your body and soul? (2 Corinthians 7:1).

4. Describe someone you know who is modest and discreet and beautiful. What can you learn from her?

5. Write out a prayer to God about what He is teaching you about inner beauty.

She is clothed with strength and dignity;
she can laugh at the days to come.

PROVERBS 31:25

Conclusion

I t had been a bad day—a very bad day. It started in the early morning as I was making French toast for our breakfast. One of the children accidentally placed a fresh loaf of bread on a hot burner while making sandwiches for lunch. Soon the smell of burning plastic filled our kitchen. What a gooey, smoky mess!

It ended late at night—after work and dinner and a middle school band concert and lots of elbow grease on the stovetop—as I was doing laundry in our basement. A couple of the kids were coming down for some Ping-Pong before bed. One of them brushed up against a huge glass container of apple juice which I, in one of my more brain-dead moments, had put on the shelf next to the stairway to the basement. I looked up from the washer to see the kids chasing the bouncing glass jug all the way down the stairs. In dreamlike slow motion, I started running for it as well, all to no avail. Before anyone could catch it, the jar had crashed onto the cement floor, sending sticky apple juice and shattered pieces of glass in all directions. At this point, I was more of a mess than the floor was. I was not clothed with strength. I was certainly not clothed with dignity.

And I was defintely not laughing. I was tired and cranky and in tears.

Match the Moment in Which You Live

Fearless femininity is tested in the *moments* of life. In our day-to-day living, we want to be women who match the moment with fearless femininity. This involves a daily choice to trust God completely. This means that whether we are mopping up apple juice and glass shards, repairing a damaged relationship, or struggling to comprehend those devastating test results in our doctor's office, God calls us to respond with strength and dignity and a settled expectancy about the days ahead.

If we want to go forward with the grace and power of fearless femininity, we must not be like those in Jeremiah's day who "did not listen or pay attention; instead, they followed the stubborn inclinations of their evil hearts. They went backward and not forward" (Jeremiah 7:24). To go backward means to "give way" to our fears (1 Peter 3:6); to let the evil of our popular culture dirty our souls with its filth; to fritter our time away on materialistic pursuits and silly entertainments; to give our husbands and children and homes a back row seat while we strive to maintain a center stage image; and to forget that heaven is real and our choices now have eternal consequences. We must not go backward! For the sake of our Lord, our families, and our communities, we must go forward into fearless femininity.

We must be women who will live for Christ, serving Him boldly. This will not be a one-time decision, but moment-by-moment choices. It will not be recognized on the six o'clock news, but it will be applauded in heaven. Why not set a new tone for the world today marked by fearless tranquility, holiness, and prayer? Why not devote ourselves to that which will strengthen the faith of families and advance the cause of Christ in our homes, neighborhoods, communities, churches, and the world?

The Only Proper Fear

In your deepest intentions, isn't this what you long to do? The only way to leave your fears and follow God's call to trust and obey and rejoice is to believe that there is only one *proper* fear: *the fear of the Lord*. Psalm 112 tells us, "Blessed is the man who fears the LORD.... His children will be mighty in the land.... He will have no fear of bad news; his heart is steadfast, trusting in the LORD. His heart is secure, he will have no fear." Fearing the Lord is the bulwark between your heart and the stubborn fears that come knocking. Knowing God, trusting His kind intentions toward you, fearing Him alone, will nurture fearless femininity in your inmost being. Then storms can blow all around you without ever ruffling the serene core of your feminine soul.

The enemies of God want to destroy the power of a Christian woman to use her femininity for Christ and His kingdom. The devil wants you to doubt God and let fears rule your heart. He hates fearless femininity. But God loves it and is committed to supporting it.

To be fearlessly feminine is to be "clothed with strength" (Proverbs 31:25). This kind of woman is strong to nurture the young and innocent and to love her husband. She is strong to give life and to care for the needs of others. She is strong to pass God's truths to the next generation. She has a womanly godliness that a man can never show. When we are clothed with strength, we become women of great influence.

Femininity is powerful in its sympathy, forbearance, and nurturing.

Let's trust God enough to fulfill His mission for us and rise from our cowardly, cultural selfism. Surrender to your God-given femininity. Don't be afraid of the call to be fearlessly feminine. Care for the next generation enough to yield your *own* desires to the one who "will give you the desires of your heart" (Psalm 37:4).

Abandon *your* personal rights *to God*. "In repentance and rest is your salvation, in quietness and trust is your strength" (Isaiah 30:15). Give yourself away in trust to God. The world tells you to close in, preserving yourself. But don't listen to its call. Don't be like the mockingbird I can hear right now outside our back window, imitating any call it hears. Follow Christ and Christ alone.

The fearlessly feminine woman is also a woman of dignity. "She is clothed with strength and dignity; she can laugh at the days to come" (Proverbs 31:25). She is poised and serene, living above the hassles of the daily grind. She continues to cast her cares on Christ because she truly believes that He cares for her (1 Peter 5:7). She is dignified because her confidence is in the God who remembers (Hebrews 6:10). She takes to heart the words in Hebrews 10:35–36: "So do not throw away your confidence; it will be richly rewarded. You need to persevere so that when you have done the will of God, you will receive what he has promised." She lets God be God! She lives in dignified peace because the Lord of peace Himself is with her, giving her peace at all times and in every situation (2 Thessalonians 3:16). She is joyfully confident in who she is as a woman before God. That strength and confidence and spirit of contentment make her fearlessly feminine.

Rejoice in Your Femininity

God made you a woman. He delights in your womanhood. Bask in the certainty that your femininity is beautiful to God. That which makes you different from the men in this world is a God-given gift, precious in His sight. Women have already proven that they can go wherever men go: space, politics, war, the boardroom. Use your femininity to go where men *cannot* go. Where is it that God is calling you to be fearlessly feminine? What is it that God created *you* for, in all your delightful femininity? What is He asking of you *as a woman?* Where does He want your feminine touch to bring strength and dignity and beauty and peace?

To clothe yourself with strength and dignity is God's call into fearlessness. It means a deep, personal fellowship with the one who created you feminine. You honor Him as you rejoice in His work. You will leave a legacy of spiritual courage as you shape a godly atmosphere in your home. Your physical strength will set an example that affirms life as you work hard at all the challenges you face. And you will enrich those around you with emotional stability as you love and teach and nurture them.

As Christian women, as Christian wives, as Christian mothers, as Christian grandmothers and aunts, as Christian employers and employees, we have the responsibility to show the next generation a clear picture of what it means to be fearlessly feminine. The image has almost faded. For those who are confused by feminist ideology, will you be fearlessly feminine? For those who need a visual model of boldly living God's plan for womanhood, will you be fearlessly feminine? For the sake of the lost world that needs the gospel, will you be fearlessly feminine? It is a privilege to obey God's call. Welcome His call to you, His daughter.

In the northeast corner of Scotland there flows a beautiful river running from the Cairngorm Mountains in the west to the North Sea in the east. It is called the River Dee. My favorite spot along this river is the Linn of Dee. There the river narrows to wind its way through a cramped rocky gorge before pushing on toward the sea. Over the years the water has smoothed the craggy rocks of the Linn. Fluid and flexible, yet strong and constant, the water shapes each rock it touches on its path to the sea. We women can be like the water flowing through the Linn of Dee as we press on with strength and dignity. As we go, let's shape our generation with the gentle but enduring touch of fearless femininity. Let's be courageous as we lift high our noble call to womanhood. Let's trust God beyond what seems possible to us.

Will you join me? Despite what the world is telling you and sometimes even your own fears, will you bless the world with the gift of your femininity? Will you be fearlessly feminine?

If God is calling you to walk down new avenues of fearless femininity, I would love to hear from you. Please let me know what God is doing in your life. You can reach me through:

Renewal Ministries
4500 Campus Drive, Suite 662
Newport Beach, California
92660

Sweet Sacrifices: A Word to Ministry Wives

He who finds a wife finds what is good
and receives favor from the LORD.
PROVERBS 18:22

M y heart is reaching out to those of you reading my
book who are involved, as I am, in full-time ministry.
Some of you married never dreaming you would hear
those six scary words: "I want to go to seminary." Others of you
knew from the beginning of your relationship that God had
called your husband into full-time Christian work. A few of
you even looked for a man to marry who had already declared
his intention to devote himself to serving Christ through the
pastorate or missions. No matter how you landed in your present position, I want to encourage you in your call to love your
husband and care for your marriage and ministry with fearless
femininity.

Perhaps you are reading this and your husband has a secular
job but also ministers extensively through lay leadership on various boards in your church or with Gideon's International or vol-
unteers with the youth or leads Bible studies or Sunday school

ministries or ministers in some other way. I hope that this chapter will encourage you as well.

When I think of wives who support their husbands in ministry, I think of a story Dr. Howard Hendricks told Ray years ago. Ray had asked him how his family dealt with his frequent travels. Dr. Hendricks replied, "My wife, Jeanne, is the key. I remember one time in particular when she was dropping me off at the airport. As I got out of the car, she turned and said to our kids, 'Aren't we lucky to be able to share our daddy with other people?' What a send-off!"

Contrast that to a comment I once heard a minister's wife make: "Clergy ought to be celibate because no decent, right-minded man ought to have the effrontery to ask any woman to take on such a lousy job! It is thoroughly un-Christian!" I wonder if you've ever felt that way? The world around you might have you believe that you are missing out on life. But I want you to know that God has called you to it. And there is no greater blessing in life than to cheerfully and wholeheartedly follow the one who created and called you and is now actively involved in sustaining you in your calling (Psalm 91:14–15; 1 Thessalonians 5:24).

God's Favor to Your Husband

When God created your husband and set him apart for the ministry, you were also part of the picture. God was thinking, "How can I encourage this servant of mine? What can I give him to help him fulfill my plan for him?" And then God created you and brought you to your man. God has "favored" your husband with *you* (Proverbs 18:22). God uses you to show your husband His grace. How? By bringing the love, acceptance, joy, and hope that only a fearlessly feminine wife can bring to a marriage. You have the unique honor of knowing intimately a man who is pressing hard to gain knowledge of God and His Word. You have the privilege of serving God along with your husband throughout your lifetime together.

Being married to someone who is devoted to ministry as his life's calling will require more of you than many other callings. There will be sacrifices you will be asked to make for the sake of the kingdom. Often they will be sacrifices that no one but God knows about. But He will be pleased to honor you for them. His loving intention is to reward you for your obedient responses to His special call upon your life (Hebrews 6:10).

If you are going to devote yourself to helping your husband, you may not have the options that open up more readily to some other wives. As early as seminary you may experience some of these limitations. Perhaps your husband is in seminary right now. This is a very unique time in your life. Your husband is very likely dealing with

- the staggering impact of concentrated study in God's Word day after day,
- the solemn responsibility of learning to interpret the Word of God accurately,
- and possibly the humbling experience of not being the primary breadwinner.

And you may be dealing with

- the intimidating reality of a widening educational gap,
- the melancholy prospect of lonely hours while he is studying,

• and the unsettling tension of abnormal financial arrange-
ments.

If you are in seminary, or if you are waiting for your next
call or your support to come in, let me urge you to never just
bide your time. Rather, embrace your present experience. Enter
into each day wholeheartedly. Don't hold back. Live boldly. You
are following God and building for eternity. Commit yourself
to embrace all that God has for you today. Don't waste your
time living in your dreams for the future. Jim Elliot, one of the
five young missionaries martyred in Equador in 1956 said,
"Wherever you are, be all there." What part of the "there"
where God has placed you are you resisting?

Don't Pamper Yourself

God has called *you* as well as your husband. He has you right
where He wants you for His glory and your happiness. He will
reward you for serving Him "with all your heart" (Colossians
3:23–24). Why do you think God has you where He does right
now? How does He want you to spend yourself joyfully at this
stage in your life? Don't adopt the mindset of the world that
tells you to look out for yourself and take it easy. That isn't
scriptural. The Bible will never tell you to pamper yourself. On
the contrary, God's Word praises hard work (Romans 16:3,
12–13; Phillipians 2:29–30). You have only a few short
decades to give yourself to the work of the Lord, and then all
eternity to enjoy your rewards. Give yourself fully to the work
of the Lord today. Abound in it, overflow, excel. God will give
value and worth to all that you do for Him. Your "labor in the
Lord" is never in vain (1 Corinthians 15:58).

You have a unique privilege as a ministry wife. God has chosen you to spend your life with one of His leaders in His kingdom work. You get to live up close with a man who has committed his life to serving others. Proverbs 3:32–33 tell us that "The LORD...takes the upright [man] into his confidence.... He blesses the home of the righteous." You get to see your husband live out what he preaches and teaches to others. You are the one who will comfort and counsel him. You are the one he will turn to for strength and encouragement and cheer. God is calling you to attend to the affairs of the kingdom with him: teaching, sharing, showing hospitality, being there in the joys and sorrows of life as you help him shepherd the flock. What an honor! What other occupation offers these privileges?

Value His Labors

The greatest thing you can do for your husband is to respect his work, to value his labor for the Lord. Pray for him. Observe him carefully. Identify with him. Cultivate ESP with him. Learn to know him better than anyone else. While my husband was teaching at Trinity Evangelical Divinity School, we came to appreciate how vital a strong marriage is to a student's degree program and future ministry. Those men whose wives entered into their seminary experience wholeheartedly were better able to develop their gifts during these important years. Their wives were fearless enough to set their husbands free to give themselves enthusiastically to their work.

I remember one wife in particular. Her husband was a Hebrew major, and she decided to take Ray's summer Hebrew class (nicknamed "killer Hebrew" by the students because of the rigorous nature of the course). Students were subjected to intensive study for six weeks. The classwork was demanding, and the homework assignments were heavy. Many students were overwhelmed.

The surprising thing was that Ray's top student in the class was this student's wife. She consistently earned straight As, despite mothering her two young children when class was over so that her husband could go to work. Oh, I almost forgot to mention that she was one of our international students and was still learning English as well! When someone asked her why she was taking on such a tough project, she replied, "I love God, and I love my husband. I want to learn what he loves."

Your husband needs you. He needs your participation in his ministry. He needs you to understand and respect the importance of his work. He needs you to free him to give his all to his calling. How can you do this?

Show appreciation and loyalty for what he does. Men in the ministry are always under fire. Keep your criticism to a minimum. He may be all too aware of his shortcomings. He needs to sense your approval. Remember Ephesian4:29: "Do not let any unwholesome talk come out of your mouths, but only what is helpful for building others up."

Develop a responsive heart. Your husband's well-being is directly related to the way you respond to him. Are you an eager listener? Do you only hear his words, or do you understand the meaning behind them? The greatest thing you can do for your husband is to listen *with understanding.* Is it safe for him to be open and innovative with you? Does he find in you a ready and willing friend, or is he unable to truly bare his soul to you?

A heavy responsibility rests on the shoulders of our men

who minister. Their sacred calling exposes them to special temptations from which other men are exempt. Often their duties draw them away from a personal enjoyment of the truth they so diligently seek to offer to others. They are deeply involved in the personal problems of their flock, and their hearts take on the wounds of their sheep. They struggle to present the gospel in compelling ways to those they see dying around them. A ministry marriage needs a wife who is responsive to these needs in her husband.

Rest content in Jesus. Your husband needs to know that you are happy to follow the Savior. He needs a wife contented in the Lord. Settle down deeply and rejoice in where God has you. He makes no mistakes. Welcome your role as a ministry wife as directly from God's hand.

Cultivate a deep intimacy with your husband that binds his heart to yours. This needs to be both emotional and physical. Intimacy must be cultivated, or it will decompose. To cultivate anything takes work. It takes time and creativity and initiative. But it will be worth it. Anything that is good takes time. As Ray's parents have written in *You Don't Have to Quit:* "Almost anything that's terrific today, earlier wasn't.

- Any marriage.
- Any church.
- Any business.
- Any person!
- Any grape. Tomato. You name it.
- Good things take time before they're good."[1]

For any marriage to be truly intimate, truly happy, the couple must know each other well and accept each other completely.

This will take time. Use all your femininity to draw him out, and then spend your lifetime loving all that you see. And let him know you, too. Teach him how to love and comfort you. Cultivate your marriage, and you will reap the sweet fruit of intimacy. Men in ministry lead a very intense life. A strong, satisfying marriage is crucial for a rich ministry. Those of us in ministry should have the happiest, most rewarding marriages of all. The world needs fearlessly feminine wives intimately involved in solid, romantic, godly marriages.

Your Heart—A Storehouse of Good Things

God is calling you not only to make sweet sacrifices in your marriage, but also to offer to Him the sweet sacrifice of a humble heart. Circumstances don't determine your response to life. That which is stored up in your heart conditions how you see everything and how you feel about everything. Jesus said, "The good man brings good things out of the good stored up in his heart, and the evil man brings evil things out of the evil stored up in his heart. For out of the overflow of his heart his mouth speaks" (Luke 6:45). What is flowing out of your heart right now as you read?

There are struggles in the ministry. There are the years of graduate study and sometimes post-graduate study that drain your financial resources while your peers start up the pay scales in their professions. There are the lonely Saturdays when your husband is studying and preparing while other families are spending time together. There are the holidays when your husband is speaking, and you wish that he could take the day off with your family. Even with one day off each week, there are the inevitable feelings of envy toward those who work a five-day week. There are the hurtful criticisms that you carry in your heart, sometimes even after your husband has forgotten them. How can we store good in our hearts for the various struggles we are sure to face as we seek to free our husbands to minister with our blessing?

Nurture Your Inner Life

First of all, nurture your inner life. Through the years it will be your relationship with your heavenly Father that will carry you through the particular difficulties of a ministry marriage. God will be the one who will listen to your cries for help, comfort you when you are discouraged, lovingly chasten you when you are self-absorbed, and meet those needs that even the most loving of husbands is unable to help a wife bear. Put God first in your life. Put Him before your husband and your children and the demands of your ministry. Let your soul find rest in Him alone (Psalm 62:1). Stay close to Him, and He will uphold you (Psalm 63:8). Wrap yourself securely in the truths of Scripture, nurturing your relationship with God. He is able to carry you through the storms of life.

A few years ago the basement in our home in Illinois flooded. As Ray and I waded through the muck, I was dismayed to see the box in which my wedding dress had been stored floating in the dirty water. Too disheartened to open the box, I tossed it on top of our Ping-Pong table and carried on with the cleanup. I let it sit there for several days, avoiding the heartbreak that was sure to set in when I had to assess the damage the flood must have caused this sentimental treasure.

Finally, I decided I had to open it and throw it out or try to redeem what was left of it. I lifted off the lid and laid the water-stained cardboard to the side. Then I started to peel off a plastic wrap that was caked with mud. I was surprised to find another layer underneath that top layer of plastic, and I kept unwrapping. My heart began to lift as I realized that this dress had been professionally wrapped, sealed securely by many layers of waterproof materials. When I finally got down to the last layer, there was my twenty-five-year-old gown, totally untouched by all the filth and water it had been floating in. In the same way, your inner life must be protected against the storms you will face in ministry. With what are you layering your soul day after day? To be fearlessly feminine in our ministry marriages, we must nurture our inner lives.

Accept the Role of a Servant

Second, accept the role of a servant. Jesus tells us, "So you also, when you have done everything you were told to do, should say, 'We are unworthy servants; we have only done our duty'" (Luke 17:10). The hardest thing about being a servant is that it's so constant, so daily, so wearing. But it is *only* hard work! What makes servanthood difficult is our expectation that we will soon leave serving and enter an easier phase of life. We tend to think

- when I get married, my problems will be solved
- or when I have children and can stay home with them, my life won't be so scattered
- or when the kids go to school, things will lighten up
- or when the kids get through these teen years, I won't be so exhausted

- or when we're not working so hard to get them through college, I'll be less stressed
- or—well, you get the picture.

We are called to serve. We are called to serve all our lives long. We are called to serve without complaint or pride. To be in ministry is to devote your life to service. Ask God to help you to "hold fast to him and to serve him with all your heart and all your soul" (Joshua 22:5).

Learn To Be a Sarah

Third, learn to be a Sarah. Don't give way to your fears (1 Peter 3:6). Many of you have left much to support your husband and minister by his side: family, jobs, homes, country, and culture. And I know that there are fears that may be assaulting your faith:

- Did I marry the wrong man?
- Do I have what it takes to make it in ministry?
- Will we make enough money?
- Will our children suffer?
- Will it really be worth it?

But fear does us no good. It paralyzes us within a web of doubt and self-absorption. It keeps us second-guessing yesterday. It breeds worry about tomorrow. And in the process, it robs us of the most important part of ministry—today! Don't let fear rob your marriage and your ministry of all that God has for you. Ask God for fearless femininity as you minister for Him. Do what is right and leave all the outcomes to His Fatherly tending.

What sweet sacrifices is God asking of you as you seek to be a fearlessly feminine ministry wife? The following poem by Amy Carmichael has encouraged me when I have felt weary or disappointed or dull of spirit. May it help you, too.

From prayer that asks that I may be
Sheltered from winds that beat on Thee,
From fearing when I should aspire,
From faltering when I should climb higher,
From silken self, O Captain free
Thy soldier who would follow Thee.

From subtle love of softening things,
From easy choices, weakenings,
(Not thus are spirits fortified,
Not this way went the Crucified,)
From all that dims Thy Calvary,
O Lamb of God, deliver me.

Give me the love that leads the way,
The faith that nothing can dismay
The hope no disappointments tire
The passion that will burn like fire,
Let me not sink to be a clod:
Make me Thy fuel, Flame of God.[2]

What easy choices and weakening things subvert you in your role as helpmeet? Are you willing to be God's fuel in your husband's ministry? Following the way of the Crucified will make you fearlessly feminine.

Study Questions

1. If you are studying this book with others, encourage the ministry wives in your group to share how they came to marry a minister.

2. Where is it hard for you to "be all there"? What promise in Scripture can encourage you to give yourself more fully?

3. Describe your greatest ministry joys.

4. How does your husband need more encouragement? How can you build more intimacy into your marriage?

5. In what ways are you layering your soul for the storms of life?

CHAPTER ONE

1. Paul Hiebert, "Mission to Hindu Women: Pandita Ramabai," in *Ambassadors for Christ,* ed. John Woodbridge (Chicago: Moody Press, 1994), 170.

2. Ibid., 173.

3. John Piper, *Recovering Biblical Manhood and Womanhood* (Wheaton, Ill.: Crossway, 1991), 46.

4. Sermon preached at the First Presbyterian Church, Augusta, Ga., 13 June 1999.

5. For further reading on this see Anne Ortlund, *Disciplines of the Heart* (Dallas: Word, 1987).

CHAPTER TWO

1. Kim Lawton, "Against the Odds," *Today's Christian Woman,* July/August 1989, 22.

2. Ibid., 56.

3. Carolyn Graglia, *Domestic Tranquility* (Dallas: Spence Publishing Co., 1998), 23.

4. Robert H. Bork, *Slouching Towards Gomorrah* (New York: HarperCollins, 1996), 204, 223.

5. Ibid., 103, 155.

6. Robert N. Munsch, *The Paper Bag Princess* (Toronto: Annick Press, 1980).

7. Babette Cole, *Princess Smartypants* (New York: Putnam, 1986).

8. Elisabeth Elliot, *Let Me Be a Woman* (Wheaton, Ill.: Tyndale House, 1976), 54.

9. Bork, *Slouching Towards Gomorrah,* 132.

CHAPTER THREE

1. Kenneth Osbeck, *Amazing Grace* (Grand Rapids: Kregel, 1990), 92.

2. Richard Stanislaw, "To God Be the Glory" in *More Than Conquerors,* ed. John Woodbridge (Chicago: Moody Press, 1992), 108.

CHAPTER FOUR

1. Ruth Graham Dienert, "Ruth Bell Graham: A Heart for the World," in *Ambassadors for Christ,* ed. John Woodbridge (Chicago: Moody Press, 1994), 65.

2. Billy Graham, *Just As I Am* (San Francisco: Zondervan, 1997), 73.

3. Ibid., 310.

4. Quoted in *Let Me Be a Woman,* by Elisabeth Elliot (Wheaton, Ill.: Tyndale House, 1976), 81.

CHAPTER FIVE

1. Gwynn Johnson, "Miss J.", in *More Than Conquerors,* ed. John Woodbridge (Chicago: Moody, 1992), 80.

2. Quoted in *Let Me Be a Woman,* by Elisabeth Elliot (Wheaton, Ill.: Tyndale House, 1976), 34.

3. Many thanks to my dear friend, Anne Morris, for her helpful insights on Hagar.

4. Margaret Clarkson, "Singleness: His Share for Me," *Christianity Today,* 23, no. 10 (16 February 1979): 15.

CHAPTER SIX

1. Mary Greetham, *Susanna Wesley, Mother of Methodism* (Great Britain: Foundry Press, 1994), 19.

2. Ibid., 22.

3. Brenda Hunter, *Where Have All the Mothers Gone?* (Grand Rapids, Mich.: Zondervan, 1982).

4. Brenda Hunter, *The Power of Mother Love* (Colorado

Springs: Waterbrook Press, 1997), 46.

5. Elizabeth Prentiss, *Stepping Heavenward* (Amityville, N.Y.: Calvary Press, 1993), 178.

6. Elisabeth Elliot, *Let Me Be a Woman* (Wheaton, Ill.: Tyndale House, 1976), 44.

7. John White, *Parents in Pain* (Madison: InterVarsity Press, 1979), 222.

8. Anne Ortlund, *Disciplines of the Home* (Dallas: Word Publishing, 1990), 79.

CHAPTER SEVEN

1. Edith Schaeffer, *The Tapestry* (Waco, Tex.: Word Books, 1981), 107.

2. Edith Schaeffer, *L'Abri* (Wheaton, Ill.: Tyndale House, 1969), 124.

3. Paul Hiebert, "Mission to Hindu Women: Pandita Ramabai," in *Ambassadors for Christ,* ed. John Woodbridge (Chicago:Moody Press, 1994), 248.

4. See Betty Friedan, *The Feminine Mystique* (New York: Norton & Co., 1963), 305–9.

5. Anne Ortlund, *Disciplines of the Home* (Dallas: Word Publishing, 1990), 13.

6. Arlie Hochshild, *The Second Shift: Working Parents and the Revolution at Home* (New York: Viking, 1989), 211–5.

7. F. Carolyn Graglia, *Domestic Tranquility: A Brief against Feminism* (Dallas: Spence Publishing Company, 1998), 183.

8. See Acts 18:1–4. Although Paul's chief goal was to spread the gospel through his teaching and preaching ministry, he also spent time in the trade of his training (tent making) to help care for his financial needs.

9. Edith Schaeffer, *What Is a Family?* (Old Tappan, N.J.: Revell, 1975), 153–4.

10. Anonymous, quoted in *I Read It on the Refrigerator*, ed. Annette Laplaca (Wheaton, Ill.: Harold Shaw Publishers, 1992), 64.

CHAPTER EIGHT

1. Elisabeth Elliot, *A Chance to Die* (New York: Fleming H. Revell, 1987), 99.

2. Ibid., 211.

3. Ibid., 223.

4. C.S. Lewis, *Mere Christianity* (New York: MacMillan Co., 1958), 49.

5. The Westminster Confession of Faith, XVI, 2.

6. *One Hundred and One Famous Poems,* comp. Roy J. Cook (Chicago: The Reilly & Lee Co., 1958), 37. Used by permission.

CHAPTER NINE

1. Edna Gerstner, *Jonathan and Sarah: An Uncommon Union* (Morgan, Pa.: Soli Deo Gloria Publications, 1995), 157.

2. Ibid., 158.

3. Mona Charen, "Degrading Exhibitionism Now in Vogue," *Augusta Chronicle,* 25 July 1999.

4. John MacArthur Jr., *Different by Design* (Wheaton, Ill.: Victor Books, 1994), 87.

APPENDIX

1. Ray and Anne Ortlund, *You Don't Have to Quit* (Nashville: Thomas Nelson Publishers, 1988), 49.

2. Amy Carmichael, *Toward Jerusalem* (Fort Washington, Pa.: Christian Literature Crusade, 1977), 94. Used by permission.